UNLOCK YOUR LEADERSHIP GREATNESS

For Students

ORLANDO CEASER

Unlock Your Leadership Greatness - For Students
Copyright © 2014 Watchwell Communications, Inc.

 Watchwell
Communications, Inc.

Published by Watchwell Communications, Inc. Offices in South Barrington, IL and Chicago, IL.

Cover design and book design by Dawn Teagarden
Photography: Papadakisphotography.com
Illustrations: Mark L. Demel

ISBN: 978-0-9960097-2-0

Library of Congress Cataloging-in-Publication Data Applied For

Ordering information for print editions:
Special discounts are available on quantity purchases by corporations, associations and educational institutions. For details regarding bulk sales inquiries for this book and other publications by the author, contact:

Orlando Ceaser
orlando.ceaser@watchwellinc.com
Tel: 847-812-5006 (mobile)
Watchwell Communications, Inc.
5 Gregory Lane
South Barrington, IL 60010
847-812-5006
224-848-4074 (fax)
www.OrlandoCeaser.com
www.watchwellinc.com
www.ozoneleadership.com

Printed in the United States of America

Dedication

To the next generations of students who are working hard to understand the world and their place in it. By unlocking their leadership greatness, they will be able to influence the world and make it a better place, one person at a time.

ACKNOWLEDGMENTS

I offer my appreciation to the numerous coaching clients who sought guidance and provided their perspectives on their needs to be more effective in school and in their work lives.

I am indebted to the Chicago City Colleges and The Black Star Project for the opportunity to work within the Chicago Public Schools system to inspire students to achieve greatness. I thank Phillip Jackson for connecting me with various organizations and for inviting me on his radio program at WVON to speak about excellence in education and to discuss my book Unlock Your Leadership Greatness.

I also benefited from connections made through the Alumni Association at Bradley University, as well as the Bradley University Black Alumni Alliance (BUBAA).

I am thankful for the many lessons I learned during my years of volunteering for the National Urban League through their Black Executive Exchange Program (BEEP). This program is a business-focused program directed at students in the Historical Black Colleges and Universities network.

I offer kudos to Scott Peterson at Willow Creek Community Church for providing a vehicle to travel to, and work with students in, the Republic of Zambia in Southern Africa. I was able to discuss with them the state of their communities and the responsibilities of students to work hard to achieve their best.

Alpha Kappa Alpha sorority, Delta Sigma Theta sorority, Omega Psi Phi fraternity and 100 Black Men were instrumental in helping me develop many of the concepts included in this book.

CONTENTS

FOREWORD

Orlando Ceaser is a wonder of the world. He has written several monumental books that focus on growth of the human spirit, intellect, and an overall ethic of care. *Unlock Your Leadership Greatness for Students* continues that work for a new era of individual: The Millenial.

As an incredible speaker and writer, Mr. Ceaser fosters a deep message in an approachable packaged format for reaching young people. He is constant and inviting in this method of leading young people to leadership greatness. Mr. Ceaser's method is one of short, calculated, deliberate steps to becoming the true definition of a purposeful leader. He asks young people, "Will you fight harder than anyone else to get what you deserve?" This becomes a pivotal tenet in the work we all have to do to get better and to succeed.

Unlock Your Leadership Greatness for Students also points students toward having goals that lead from a dream. So often, we rely on the world to take care of us, but difficulties will ensue if you choose not to heed Mr. Ceaser's chapter called, "Powered by a Dream." The curriculum of life is easy to stray away from if the dream doesn't have adequate global positioning systems. Mr. Ceaser grinds at the importance of having dreams, goals, purposes, actions, and plans, in order to attain and maintain accomplishment.

Mr. Ceaser brings Dr. Philip Zimbardo and Malcolm Gladwell into the conversation for young people. Mastering a skill isn't rocket science nor brain surgery, however, Mr. Ceaser's approach emphasizes the element of persistence. He drives the point to students that persistence in your skill will lead to mastery, and that mastery comes from putting in your 10,000 hours.

With anagrams, acronyms, and clever alliterations, *Unlock Your Leadership Greatness for Students* makes reading an enjoyable experience for those students who want to improve their performance in school and in professional environments.

Mr. Ceaser is genius at creating page turners. It's always fun to read an Orlando Ceaser book, because he will entertain the reader while providing meaningful lessons and strategies for success. Trying to teach Abraham Maslow's hierarchy of needs to students is tough. But Ceaser does it skillfully.

Orlando Ceaser wants students to "Always Be Creative" and with this book, his readers will rise to the occasion and surpass their expectations by using mind skills that they have never before used. This is a must read for young people who truly want to unlock their leadership greatness.

Garrard McClendon, Ph.D.
Professor, Author, Talk Show Host

PREFACE

You are among the untold millions of individuals in our known universe who seek information, knowledge and wisdom through various methods. You will invoke the changes you need to see in the world. You will stoke the fires of revolution, initiate uprisings in countries around the world and march against perceived injustices in government and institutions. Your political activism is similar to that of the 1960s: impassioned and unyielding. Your creativity in the arts and sciences is undeniable. Your discontent with the status quo is a marker for change. Flash mobs and the social media explosion are examples of your ingenuity.

You are the life long, continuous learners who strive to improve yourselves, the human condition and your environment. You are the next generation of leaders. Leadership involves influencing others and serving as a role model to peers and people who look up to you. Leadership development is achieved through constant stimulation and simulations. Your adventure is magnified as you reach out and explore your world, consuming messages and morsels of data in a satisfying quest for leadership greatness.

You relentlessly expand your intellect, which further enriches the range of your conversations. You know that you must grow in order to live fully. You know that the nuts and bolts of your education is only enhanced by your powers of observation and the use of your other senses. While still gaining new knowledge, your mind is energized as you move toward enlightenment and fulfillment.

You are students of the game of life, students of your craft and talent and students who evaluate yourselves and others. You spend time studying your future occupation and the forces that influence your relationships. In this book, you will explore 10 practical principles. Each key will direct your thinking and guide your focus on the path to unlock your leadership greatness. The ten keys evolved from over three decades of my experience in observing and developing Impact Players. In sports, the Impact Players are the difference makers, the people who change the outcome of the game and inspire higher performances from their peers. We can all be Impact Players in our chosen fields.

Leadership is an expectation you should have for yourself. The world is confident you will display leadership qualities to direct nations into a brave new world. Your values and beliefs, expectations, behavior, environment and level of engagement are directly linked to results you will deliver. This relationship is outlined in the leadership continuum below.

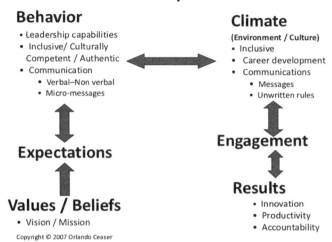

Leadership Continuum

Behavior
- Leadership capabilities
- Inclusive/ Culturally
  Competent / Authentic
- Communication
  - Verbal–Non verbal
  - Micro-messages

Expectations

Values / Beliefs
- Vision / Mission

Copyright © 2007 Orlando Ceaser

Climate
(Environment / Culture)
- Inclusive
- Career development
- Communications
  - Messages
  - Unwritten rules

Engagement

Results
- Innovation
- Productivity
- Accountability

An invaluable asset for today's leaders is the ability to think critically. You should always focus on critical thinking. Do not take this gift for granted. Everyone thinks, although some seem to do it more than others do and some do not seem to do it very well. Thinking is a skill you can develop. Schools should offer a class called, "How to improve your thinking skills." Everyone could benefit from such a class. Since such a class does not exist, you must develop your own thinking skills. Statistics indicate that the highest achievers only use 5 to 10% of their thinking capacity. Therefore, even those who have a reputation as deeper thinkers or great minds only scratch the surface of their potential. If this is true, everyone has room to grow. If someone says that you cannot handle something or you doubt your ability to think, remember you have more than enough capacity. Your power to think and reason, together with your desire and discipline to excel, will propel you to the next level of leadership.

The future and the stability of this planet, its countries and communities, as well as relationships of all kind, depend on students unlocking their leadership greatness. Never before has the need been so important for you to study leadership. You must harness the power of leadership. Unlock and unleash your potential.

CHAPTER 1

BE FIT FOR THE ROLE

Excel in areas where you can fully utilize your talents, skills and abilities

"A musician must make music, an artist must paint, a poet must write, if he is to be ultimately at peace with himself. What a man can be, he must be."

—Abraham Maslow

"I feel pressure from my purpose, to align my passion with my potential."

—Orlando Ceaser

"Find out what you like doing best and get someone to pay you for doing it."

—Katherine Whitehorn

Who Are You?

Who are you? You may answer this question in many ways. You may state your name. You may follow-up with being the son or daughter of your parents. Your family association, community, village or country may be a part of your personal definition. You may identify with a certain race, culture, country or ethnic group.

Who are you? You may answer that you are a member of the human race. You are more like others than you are different. The Human Genome Project says humans are 99.1% alike through our genes.[1] Scientists can trace all of us back through the gene pool to a part of Africa.[2] Although everyone is similar, fingerprints and brain waves demonstrate that each of us is unique. You have talents, skills and abilities that are encoded in you. There are things that come easily to you because you were made to do them well. Further, there are talents that you can improve upon through practice and hard work.

The minerals in you have a value of approximately $4.50,[3] but your intellect, spirit, relational ability and compassion are priceless. You are unique, special and one of a kind. Sure, you are connected to all people, related to everyone, but you are a separate individual with perspective and input that only you can provide. You are too important to not fully develop yourself and find your purpose and potential.

You have the ability to reason, to think and to love, with a higher level of consciousness than animals. You can show compassion, mercy and creativity. Who are you? To answer the question thoroughly you need to explore the visual, physical, mental and spiritual. This will give you a greater awareness of your identity.

You may have learned to define yourself with external markers, i.e., the items that you possess, the things that you do, or others' opinions of you. If you believe your identity is tied to your possessions, then it naturally follows that if you are not wealthy and possess only limited material objects, you are nobody. When you are in this state of limited means, you will have a lower opinion of yourself. The underlying message, according to Dr. Wayne Dwyer, is "If we are what we have, then when we don't have, we aren't."[4] Using this concept, everyone would allow their current state to define their lives. The rich may believe they are more valuable to society, while the poor may feel as if they have no voice and are of little consequence. This thought pattern is self-limiting and you must reject it so that you can continue to live your purpose, no matter the size of your bank account.

If you tie your identity to what you do (e.g., your job as company manager or your role as the captain of your school's softball team), you run a similar risk of your identity being affected negatively in the event of any status change. If you lose your job, experience a demotion, or fail to win re-election as the student body president, then you are nobody. In reality, you are more than what you do. A change in status at work, school or any other area of your life should provide a different opportunity, not a different identity.

If your identity is linked to what others think of you, you may find your sense of identity in constant flux. You will constantly seek the opinions of others, shifting your image to gain their approval. Depending upon your ability to meet others' approval, you may find that your self-esteem is also on a roller coaster ride.

Another drawback of basing your self-identity on the opinions of others is that their opinions may have a toxic origin. Based upon their own negative outlook, some will try to define you and lump you into a category based on their thoughts of you. Who are you?

They will answer the question in a way that is not constructive for you. Their answer may draw upon their own insecurities, often based on the notion that we are defined by our wealth or status. By internalizing others' negativity, you may find that your sense of self worth is compromised and you may not reach for the higher goal. If, however, you are grounded in who you really are, your self-identity and self-esteem will come from within, a more reliable and energizing source of strength.

You should not define yourself based on what you own, what you do or what others think of you. Dr. Dwyer says we should get to the point where we believe who we are has value, because we exist.[5]

When you were born, your parents likely looked into your eyes and said or thought, "You are beautiful. I love you. Someday you will have a positive impact on the world. You will contribute to this family in a very special way." You entered a world with a lot of hype, a lot of hope and high expectations around your arrival and your participation. These great and positive expectations are the promise you are destined to fulfill.

I recall something my mother used to say to me. "You are the chosen one," she said. My response was "chosen by whom, to do what or for what purpose?" She told me the story of the children of Israel. She told me about how, according to the Hebrew people, they were the chosen ones of God. God was part of the answer, but the riddle was in the second half of the question. It was up to me to find out what He wanted me to be from the many clues He planted in my life.

You are the chosen one, each of you. You have a purpose, a reason for being here. Do you know what it is? How are you going down the path of discovery? Have you tried to find your purpose?

You are not an accident. You are a necessary piece of the puzzle of life. The world's potential is realized through you. In fact, you have defied the odds. You are intentional. Someone wanted you to be here. You overcame probability and the law of averages to be in a position to contribute to the universe.

You may be in the early years of adulthood, possibly thinking of acquiring credit to purchase your necessary material possessions. At this stage, you have no doubt encountered information on the prevalence and dangers of identity theft. An entire industry has sprung up where companies are selling you insurance in the event of identity theft. Identity theft is a major issue as people try to exploit you. However, you are responsible for preventing another, more dangerous, crime: Identity Surrender.

Identity Surrender occurs when you are not being your true self and living without your purpose and full potential as your guide. You may unwittingly assume the identity of some idealized person whose motivations and aspirations are not your own. Ordinarily, you will resist when people try to convince you to abandon your principles and take on their actions and points of view. However, this may prove difficult to do in certain circumstances, especially when you find yourself in a new peer group. You may give in, give up and give away who you are, because you are not prepared to fight for your position. You may not have enough confidence in yourself to fight for your "self" as defined by you. Do not let this happen. You need to unlock your leadership greatness and make a positive and significant impact on the world.

Finding Your Fit

Cocky & Rhodette   by Orlando Ceaser

Many times in your life, you have tried to fit in. You wanted to fit in with a certain crowd because of prestige and notoriety. Fitting in socially will always be a mission for many of us, but soon you will be in the process of determining where you fit in vocationally. Exploring your talent, skills and abilities may reveal an aptitude for certain occupations. For example, personality assessments such as Meyers – Briggs (MBTI) and DISC (Dominance, Influence, Steadiness, and Conscientiousness) and True Colors, will give you a personality profile.[6] Additionally, the results can lead to recommended occupations where your personality traits prove to be a good fit. These exercises can be especially helpful for those college students who are in a state of "major confusion," i.e., you are currently undecided on a major or you have spent years working toward completing a major for which you are no longer committed.

You may also select or have selected a major in college that will prepare you for a career that matches the dreams you had as a youngster. Your chosen career path may be one suggested by either your parents or popular culture or one that best ensures your financial security. No matter the reason for choosing your career path, it is crucial to pursue or select a job that matches your skills and abilities and your desire to work hard to be successful. You must select a job for which you are willing to do the work.

Furthermore, you must realize that the landscape for careers is very dynamic. Many people are enjoying exciting jobs that did not exist when they started college. Many others have changed careers after entering the workforce because they found something more suitable for their skills and interests. The key is always to keep in mind that you will be more likely to excel and derive the greatest satisfaction from your chosen profession when the fit is right. When you have the right fit, in the right job, you look forward to going to work each day.

Identity

Who decides how you feel about yourself? Do you compare yourself to others to arrive at your opinion? There is no one on the planet like you. You have your own special DNA, fingerprint and experiences. To be alive with the ability to think makes you a very sophisticated and special being.

As a public speaker, I often seek out opportunities to engage with young students. I like to deliver a call and response greeting to energize the audience. It consists of three questions:

1. Is anyone better than you are?
2. Does anyone deserve more than you deserve?
3. Will you fight harder than anyone else to get what you deserve?

Is Anyone Better Than You Are?

To my first question, the response is usually a resounding "No!" or "No way!" However, when I listen carefully and study faces, I notice that some students appear to be unsure and others actually answer "yes." I ask those students why do they feel that someone is better than they are. They usually explain that someone has more "stuff" or can do things better than they can do them. Some students mistakenly base their relative value on what they do not have. Some will even mention that they are not creative and others are more creative than they are. After a bit of conversation, all the students ultimately answer the initial question with a "No!"

Does Anyone Deserve More Than You Deserve?

The students also answer my second question with a powerful "no," with a few faint "yes" answers in the crowd. Some students have shown surprise at those who answered "yes," eyeing them as if something was wrong with them. When I explore the few faint "yeses" in the group, I hear the same kind of reasons as with the first question. However, I also gain a better sense of their values. Some of the students felt that others have less than they do and therefore deserve to have more. Interestingly, the answers to this question also reveal that the students believe that if people work harder they deserve to receive a greater reward. Generally, however, the students feel they are just as deserving as is anyone else on the planet.

Our society is full of images that may lead to a diminished sense of self worth in many people. Therefore, it may take extra effort for some people to know that they deserve just as much as the next person does. Many people feel less about themselves because they feel they have less than people in other socio-economic groups, other communities or in other parts of the world. News stories highlight such disparities as gender wage inequality, economic gaps between the rich and the poor and the relative advantages bestowed on those considered to be more physically attractive. Real and perceived disadvantages lead some to believe they are working from behind. It takes a special person with a strong mindset to work effectively when running from behind.

I ran track when I was a young man, both at the high school and collegiate level. The distance runners always fascinated me. One of my favorites was Jim Ryan. Jim would often find himself in the back of the pack, but as the race continued, he would begin to move up in the pack. Eventually, he would confidently display his "kick," which was a burst of speed to carry him toward the front of the line. I would watch him stay focused and slowly pass one runner at a time until he reached his goal. I had a fellow runner, Ramel Diab, who also had this ability to kick strongly, as he moved up in races. You would almost count Mel out of the race and then he would make his move. He would start climbing through the pack, passing each runner along the way until he raced toward a victorious finish.

If you are running from behind it requires patience and a will to keep running. Your focus should be on passing those immediately in front. They will serve as guideposts or mile markers for you. You also need encouragement along the way. Encouragement can come in many forms. It could come from a friendly group of supporters or from internal self-talk urging you to go on because you can make it. Consider the person at the front of the pack as your long-term goal. Your immediate focus and concentration should be on someone within your reach or your personal best time. Then you continue to extend your reach. Your confidence will increase each time you pass someone in front of you or each time you pass a personal goal.

It is important to work harder, study longer and receive the best coaching you can get. If someone is ahead of you because she started training earlier, then you have to be persistent to catch up by training longer and harder to reach your goal. You can also help yourself by thinking more about your goal than he is thinking about his dreams.

Will You Fight Harder Than Anyone Else to Get What You Deserve?

I ask the third question: "Will you fight harder than anyone else to get what you deserve?" Of course, the preferred answer for this question is "yes." The "yes" responses were not as emphatic and self-assured as the "no" responses in the first two questions. Somehow indicating that they may not work harder than someone else was not an embarrassing admission.

My sense is that the answer to the third question reflects a matter of choice. Everyone can make the decision, for any number of reasons, as to the amount of effort they will put into obtaining certain assets. Some may recognize that others have better grades, higher status or more wealth and material possessions. They may believe that those advantages may make it more difficult to compete with those who are better off. However, you can choose to close the gap and work harder and smarter to catch up, but it requires a plan. You determine the amount of effort and the quality of that effort. You realize that the quality of the result will be based on the amount and quality of the effort. By taking action and putting in your best effort, you are claiming the right to what you deserve.

The answers to these questions give you insight into how you feel about yourself. If given the opportunity in a public setting, many people would probably answer questions similarly to my student groups. In reality, it is likely that they would have the same insecurities as did some of those children. Unpacking and analyzing your true feelings can show you that there is room for improvement with respect to your self-image and self-esteem.

"I Am" Statements

There are habits you can adopt that will remind you of your importance. These may be familiar to you. They are affirmations and can be said daily or at other regular intervals. There are "I am" statements that you can use to help reinforce and affirm your belief in your value. You can start by writing five true statements about yourself. The statements will start with the words "I am." Below are some examples.

- I am someone whose input is valuable.
- I am creative.
- I am someone important.
- I am a leader.
- I am God's child.

- I am intelligent.
- I am special and deserve respect.
- I am my parents' treasure.
- I am someone great.
- I am someone who can be trusted.

"I am" statements can help you strengthen your identity and remind you of the awesome responsibility that rides on your shoulders. The "I am" statements must reflect how you really feel about yourself, whether you currently possess those attributes or they are attributes toward which you are striving. This feeling must be reinforced in your mind, especially in your subconscious. Your subconscious mind does a lot of your thinking. It is responsible for what people will call automatic thinking. When you recite the "I am" statements, they are stored in your subconscious mind as the truth and you will act in accordance with this reality.

You can change your beliefs if you work on them. If you consciously act as if they are true, eventually they will be true. Read the book, The Most Powerful Book of Affirmations Ever Written by Sheldon T. Ceaser, M.D.[7] It is a phenomenal source to lift your spirits and guide your thinking to a better life.

Discussions Topics for Personal Reflection and Small Groups

1. Discuss the role of your parents or guardians in shaping who you are.

2. Advertising, books, society and the media create images and expectations. Review some of the key messages about you and the groups of which you are a part.

3. Faith and religion play a role in creating identity. Review how they affect or direct your life.

4. What positive and negative influences have your friends had on your development?

5. Write your own "I am" statements and affirmations.

CHAPTER 2

BE POWERED BY A DREAM

*Be driven by ambitious and stretch goals
to fulfill your potential and purpose*

"All our dreams can come true, if we
have the courage to pursue them."

—Walt Disney

"It's not the critic who counts; not the man who points out
how the strong man stumbles, or where the doer of deeds
could have done them better. The credit belongs to the
man who is actually in the arena, whose face is marred
by dust and sweat and blood;... who at the best knows in
the end the triumph of high achievement, and who at the
worst, if he fails, at least fails while daring greatly..."

—President Theodore Roosevelt

"Don't ask yourself what the world needs; ask yourself
what makes you come alive. And then go and do
that. Because what the world needs are people
who have come alive."

—Harold Whitman

Unlocking your leadership greatness signals to the world that you are powered by a dream. Creating a vision is an essential component of leadership. Walt Disney said, "If you can dream it, you can do it." This type of innovation and belief is the fire you need to become a phenomenal leader.

People are willing to work hard for their dreams. I spent a lot of time around creative people: artists, actors, painters, models and musicians. I was amazed at their level of sacrifice and hard work in pursuit of their dreams. They worked all types of odd jobs. The jobs were usually unglamorous, low paying and completely unrelated to their dream. They did this because they were powered by a dream. Their interim status was temporary. They knew these jobs were not their destination, only a station on the railway to success.

As a student, you have chemistry, and you display a certain persona when interacting with friends and faculty within a higher learning environment. The academic setting is often a relaxed one, one where you feel free to let yourself shine. You may explore creative outlets, such as drama courses, or you may seek out leadership roles in student government. While this is a time for exploration, coming into yourself in a sense, it is also an opportunity to determine how these experiences will fit in with your plans for the future. Ideally, you will be a lifelong student in that you will always seek to learn and grow. However, your formal schooling, undergraduate and post-graduate, will be temporary and is likely to go by in the blink of an eye. The rest of your life will be filled with challenges for which you can draw upon your academic experiences. It is up to you to take what you can from student life to fulfill your real world dreams.

When you are powered by a dream, there is unlimited energy and focus to succeed. You have the sense of purpose, a sense of urgency, a higher calling for a brighter future. Think of parents who work long hours and several jobs for minimal pay so that they can provide a better life for their children. Think of the artists, models, actors and other creative individuals discussed earlier. Think of the inventors who relentlessly pursue their vision of a new product. Their dreams keep them moving, even though rewards may be far off in the future. You, too, have the capacity to be powered by a dream.

The mother of a college student asked me to speak to her son about his career aspirations. He was a freshman in college with a 3.9 grade point average. His dream was to make the world a better place through love and positivity.

I asked him a series of questions to determine if he had thought about the structure necessary to achieve his goals. The most important question was "how are you going to do that?" He said that he would become a psychologist or a psychiatrist. Again, I asked, "How are you going to do that?" He responded that he would major in psychology with a minor in philosophy.

I knew that he was an intelligent young man with noble goals, but I wanted to dig deeper to determine whether he had considered some of the real-life hurdles that he may encounter. I asked, "Just for the record, if there is a delay in going after your Masters degree, how are you going to eat? How will you afford a roof over your head and pay your bills?" I wanted to know if he had a Plan B or a contingency plan in case his original objective was delayed.

I continued. "I have seen many people's careers interrupted and they did not have a backup plan. You may want to consider business as a minor, to help you understand finances and to strengthen your profile in case you need to get a job earlier than planned. Understanding finances will also help you become a better business person, whether you are a psychologist, a psychiatrist or if you decide there is another profession you would like to pursue toward your ultimate goal of making the world a better place."

Many people are idealistic in college and that is understandable and not surprising. Your goals are lofty and you have your whole life ahead of you to make them come to fruition. However, you would benefit greatly if you take the time to incorporate real-life elements into your strategies for meeting your objectives. No matter your objective, whether it is changing the world through love and positivity or obtaining the education to secure a high earning position in the world of finance, you must consistently factor in the basics. Ask yourself, "How am I going to eat or otherwise support myself during those times before my goals have been fully realized?"

Everyone has a dream for the future. What is yours? When you unlock your leadership greatness, you will notice a fully functioning dream. You may have an over arching dream around success and your contributions to humanity. Alternatively, you may have a dream around your family and the life you wish to provide for them. Your dream may be to express a talent or skill and the good you can provide for people in need. Just as important as it is to have a dream, it is equally important to believe you have the ability to reach it. Many people give up on their dreams, possibly due to discouragement from others or because their own experiences led them to doubt their abilities. You can create hope and possibility and it begins in your mind. It is your dream and you have the power to make it reality.

Your dream should become your goal. What is a goal? A goal can be defined in different ways, depending on the context. A useful way of approaching goals is: "A goal is a dream with a deadline."[1] A dream is your goal, which should be followed by a plan and the desire to act on it. It does not take courage to dream, establish a goal or create a plan, but it does take courage to act. The choice is yours.

Explanation for Your Dream

When you have selected your dream or dreams, it is also important to ask yourself, why is this "My" dream? You may discover that you want to be a doctor because you love to help people. Someone else may want to be a pediatric nurse because she loves to work with children. When you break down a dream to its smallest parts or its very essence, you will find the real reason behind it. As a result, you may find yourself living out your dream via a different route. For example, the person who wants to be a doctor may find the cost of tuition is prohibitively expensive. Since he knew he wanted to be a doctor to help people, he may shift his career to another aspect of the medical industry that is more affordable. The person who wants to be a nurse may become a schoolteacher, a profession where she will have many opportunities to interact with children in a meaningful way. Neither has given up on their core dreams, they merely found other avenues to realize them.

By understanding the reasons behind your dreams, you have more flexibility in making your choices and tailoring your future. You will also be successful in life. You must not consider yourself a failure simply because you did not land your "dream job." Your dreams are rarely static and neither are your choices. Even further, the world we live in is ever changing. A kid in the 1960's, unless they had an unbelievable imagination, probably did not dream of being an internet superstar. Yet, today that dream is being realized on a daily basis.

Dreams can and should be grand. Do not look to careers just because they are popular. On the other hand, do not shy away from areas that require a skill you may not have fully mastered. You should base your decision on your gifts, talents and capacity for greatness. You should be guided ultimately by your dreams and whether that particular career will provide you the type of satisfaction that you deserve. As will be discussed further in this book, making your dream a reality requires real work. Therefore, you will need to hone skills along the way and that may include mastering statistics or learning how to sell products to strangers.

It is critical to allow yourself the freedom and flexibility to select and express the dreams that are within your heart. When you dream and when you have a dream, your enthusiasm for it will provide the light and energy to attract the people and resources you require. Dr. Wayne Dyer has a phrase that I think is very important to give dreamers encouragement. "The people you need and the resources you need are on the way."[2] As you work toward achieving your dream, which involves planning and executing the plan, be confident that what you need will be there to help you reach your goal.

Hunger for Greatness

An African Tale

An old African sage, wise and influential, lived on the side of a mountain near a lake. It was common practice for the people of the village to seek his advice. The old man spent many hours sitting in front of his small hut, where he rocked in a crude rocking chair made of branches and twigs. Hour after hour, he sat and rocked as he thought.

One day he noticed a young African warrior walking on the path toward his hut. The young man walked up the hill and stood erect before the sage. "What can I do for you?" the old man asked.

The warrior replied, "I was told by those in the village that you were very wise. They said you can give me the secret of happiness and success."

The old man listened, and then gazed at the ground for several moments. He rose to his feet, took the young man by the hand,

and led him down the path back toward the lake. Neither of them spoke a word. The young warrior was obviously bewildered, but the sage kept walking. Soon they approached the lake, but did not stop. Out into the water, the old man led the young man. The farther they walked, the more the water advanced. The water rose from the warrior's knees to his waist, then to his chin, but the old man said nothing and kept moving deeper and deeper. Finally, the lad was completely submerged. At this point, the wise man stopped for a moment, turned the young man around, and led him out of the lake and up the path back to the hut. Still not a word was spoken. The old man sat again in his creaky chair and rocked back and forth.

After several minutes, he looked into the warrior's questioning eyes and asked, "Young man, when you were in the lake, under water, what did you desire most?"

Openly excited, he replied, "Why, you old fool, I wanted to breathe!" Then the sage spoke these words: "My son, when you want happiness and success in life as badly as you wanted to breathe, you will have found the secret."

Willingness to Sacrifice

I spoke to a young medical doctor who told me about his early experience in college. He was a product of an inner city school system where he performed exceptionally well in his classes. When he arrived at a prestigious university, he noticed in the beginning of the semester that most students completed their assignments by studying until 9 o'clock in the evening. However, he had to work until midnight to finish his assignments. He was one of the best students in his high school, but he found himself slightly behind the other students in his classes. Most of his classmates had attended private high schools or suburban public high schools that had a greater emphasis on college preparatory work. Eventually, he caught up to his peers by making necessary sacrifices. He said he was willing to stay up as long as it took to avoid falling behind in his classes.

How much can you have if you are willing to work and wait for what you really want? You have to be willing to do the work and wait for the fruits of your labor. You must believe in the system that says you will be rewarded for your effort. The old saying is still true, "the only place success comes before work is in the dictionary."

One day my wife was complaining about the amount of weight she needed to lose. She was talking to our son and he became impatient with her never-ending dissatisfaction with her figure. At that time, my son, Brian, was a college football player. He was 6'2", weighed 255 pounds, bench pressed 475 pounds and ran the 40-yard dash in 4.6 seconds. He was a beast on the field and a first team All-American football player.

My wife said, "I have to lose weight." Brian said something to his mother that you should never say to your mother. He replied, "Obviously, you don't want it badly enough," and then he took off running. She chased him through the house. They ran up the stairs and around the house. She came to me panting and said, "Did you hear what he said to me?" I jokingly said, "My name is Les, I am not in this mess." She stopped, thought and said, "Maybe he is right. I know what I need to do to lose weight. I know how much exercise I need and how I must change my diet. Maybe I have not wanted it badly enough."

To unlock your leadership greatness, you must have a dream and a hunger for realizing your goal.

Changes and Consequences

Now you are powered by your dream, you understand why you chose the dream and you want it badly enough. What is next? Many are surprised to find that, when they are moving in a positive direction, they may get resistance from those who are closest to them. Close friends and acquaintances may react negatively toward you for reasons that are hard for you to grasp. As you change and start moving in the direction of your dream, you may give up old practices or associations that no longer fit in with your ultimate goals. Maybe your social outings will become fewer because you have a rigorous research schedule. You may find yourself spending more time with people who are pursuing similar goals. In either event, your existing base of friends will notice changes in your interactions with them. They may try to influence you to maintain the status quo. They are used to you and your relationship being a certain way and any shift will cause them to feel uncertainty. They may wonder, "Will we remain friends? Will we still have the same things in common?" Being aware of your environment and of how it will inevitably change when you change will be very important to your adjustment. You must:

- Recognize the dream or how you want to be

- Understand how you grow and map out the steps in your growth journey

- Not underestimate the pressure to return to your old ways. This pressure will come from yourself and from others

Be Powered by a Dream

Sticking with the Change

When you are changing, there is a natural tendency to doubt yourself and an urge to return to the old ways to minimize conflict and hurt feelings. You wonder if you made a mistake and if you are capable of finishing and reaching your goals. The cost of change may seem too high for you, but you must push ahead. Here are a few ideas to help keep you on track and follow through with your commitment to change:

- Use a journal to keep track of your progress
- Regularly review and report your status or progress to a confidante
- Choose a partner who shares your goals and work in tandem to keep each other on track
- Make a promise/commitment to someone secretly or make a public declaration
- Place a written note someplace where you will see it daily to remind yourself of your promise
- Check in with a coach or mentor to receive support, motivation and guidance
- Listen to music, read books and talk to people that inspire and encourage you
- Include your goals in your daily prayers and/or affirmations

41

Discussions Topics for Personal Reflection and Small Groups

1. List the top 3 dreams you plan to accomplish in your life time

2. What will you need to realize each dream? What resources will you require?

3. Who will have to play a role in your life to help make your dream a reality?

4. At what stage will you ask others for help?

5. What barriers or resistance do you expect to overcome? How will you succeed?

6. What will you do if your friends discourage you, subtly or overtly, from pursuing your dreams?

CHAPTER 3

BE A STUDENT
OF THE GAME

*Continuously learn information related to your
studies, interests and career options*

"When the student is ready, the teacher will appear."

—Ancient Sanskrit proverb

"Winning is great, sure, but if you are really going to
do something in life, the secret is learning how to lose.
Nobody goes undefeated all the time. If you can pick
up after a crushing defeat, and go on to win again, you
are going to be a champion someday."

—Wilma Rudolph

"In elephant society, younger elephants look up to
the matriarchs. Why? Because they know where
to find the water from 50 years ago."

—Temple Grandin

The Competitive Landscape

Competition is a part of your natural environment. You cannot escape it. Others will desire anything of value or that has the promise of a great reward. The most prestigious schools often have more than twenty applicants for each available spot. Similarly, job postings for the most sought after positions may generate hundreds of resume submissions. The competition is those individuals who are working toward the same goals you want to accomplish.

The competition may be students in your classroom, city or country. Competitors may be at your company, working in positions inside or outside of your profession. Competition may also be from people in remote regions of the world. Now, more than ever, competition demands that you put forth your maximum effort. The current marketplace draws on the talents found throughout this global economy. Students and professionals throughout the world want access to the riches and resources of the major markets. You have likely noticed in your life the increased demands on your time and energy. Your college professors are preparing you for the rigors of increased competition. If you are already in the workforce, the increased demands are likely a direct result of your company's recognition of how it must perform in the fiercely competitive marketplace.

Competitive Response

People respond differently to competition. When faced with competition, people respond in at least one of six ways. They will compete, concede, complain, condemn, conform or confuse.

—Compete

People who understand the competitive environment and decide to compete are ready for action. They know that they have to be in it to win it. They realize that their best performance is required to earn the prize. When medals are awarded to the best players, they want to be on the podium. They study the competition and devise plans to combat their opponent. They condition and prepare to fight as hard as necessary to win. They work on skills and standards and plan to emerge as winners. They realize the best, most gratifying result comes when they are honest and play by the rules. There are those who may use dishonest methods, but many want to compete fairly in order to achieve their goals with honor. They spend the long hours to do the work to be ready for combat.

If you have established a personal brand, you will work hard to protect your reputation for excellence. Hard work and determination are prerequisites to success. These competitors are future-focused people who recognize the effort required to be a champion. If you were going to play another team in a sporting event, what would you do to prepare? What kind of research would you do? Because you take the game seriously, you would probably:

- Conduct research on the other team to identify their key players
- Analyze their strategies and their most common plays
- Assess their strengths and weaknesses
- Look to their other competitors, study the ones who beat them and understand their game plan

You will use some of these same strategies and tactics when

planning to compete in life, whether it is in school, sports or in your career. You will know your competition and know how you need to prepare yourself to meet them head-on. This will involve tweaking your skills and performance level to be always ready for changes in the competitive landscape. By consistently improving on your previous performance, you will always grow your skills.

—Concede

It takes a great deal of energy and resolve to engage in competition. Some people lack both of those characteristics and they will instead concede defeat. The decision to retreat in the face of competition results from any number of factors. The player may believe that the competition is stronger, bigger, has many more resources or has too great of a lead. Some may feel intimidated by the amount of work necessary to reach their goal. Moreover, quite frankly, others may be too lazy to put forth the time and energy it takes to effectively compete in their chosen arena. While most people like to win, some hate to lose even more. They may choose to take themselves out of the game, whether consciously or by lack of effort, and thereby avoid the shame of losing.

The conceders are easy to identify. In the classroom, they are the ones who do not complete their assignments and appear to be unengaged during class time. Similarly, in the workplace, the conceders show up for work and just go through the motions. In regards to competitors, they will often say things such as, "I would never do that" or "I could never be like them." They are not engaged fully in their work and are the "clock-watchers," those who only put in the bare minimum until it is time to clock out for the day. In the military, they are called R.O.A.D.: Retired On Active Duty.

Another reason people may quit the race is for fear. Two sides of the same coin, fear of success and fear of failure, may lead to a diminished desire to compete. Those who are afraid of winning may put on their game face and try to project the image of someone who is actively competing. In reality, they may question their ability to maintain the work ethic and responsibility that comes with winning. Those who are afraid of failing will not give their best effort. If they do not play, they cannot lose. On the other hand, if they do play and ultimately lose, they feel comfort in knowing they did not invest fully with their time and energy. They may try to save face by saying, "I could have done it if I wanted to." Both of these groups lack the necessary confidence for continued success, which explains why they are not successful.

In order to avoid allowing your fears or any other self-limiting doubts to affect your chances for success, you must recognize that you must be in the game mentally as well as physically. If you have mentally thrown in the towel, it has a negative impact on your effort and results. If you believe there is a possibility of victory, even if slight, then you are miles ahead of someone who has mentally conceded defeat.

– Complain

A common reaction to competition is to complain. These individuals are whiners and constant complainers. They cause defeat in the hearts of their teammates or others working toward the same goal. They spend more time complaining about what is not right than thinking about a solution. They are looking for reasons to blame others when they fail at their job. It is never their fault. It is always something or someone on the outside preventing them from being successful. The negative thinking of the complainers can affect the morale of the team, causing others to lose focus and confidence.

Complaining and negativity can be very expensive. Jon Gordon, in his book The No Complaining Rule, cites statistics from the Gallup Organization that states negativity costs the U.S. economy from $250 to $300 billion every year in lost productivity. Additionally, he writes that ninety percent of doctor visits are stress related, according to the Centers for Disease Control and Prevention; and the #1 cause of office stress is co-workers and their complaining, according to Truejobs.com.[1]

If you want to accomplish a particular goal, you understand that the task may be daunting. Of course, you may want to vent along the way. That is only natural. However, if you find yourself complaining without adding value, you may need to take a step back. Not only are you losing sight of what is most important, you may also be having a negative impact on those closest to you who you will need for support and positive encouragement. Instead of complaining, ask yourself, "What do can I do about this problem? Is there a solution that will get me closer to my goal?"

— Condemn

There are individuals who condemn those striving to get results. Ridicule is a tool that they use to make fun of those trying to be successful. They look at other people and see they are performing better than they are. Rather than increase their results, they take the easy way by bringing down others. Condemners try to work on your mind, confidence and self-esteem. They accuse people of:

- Selling out

- Not playing fair
- Lacking some key ingredient of intelligence
- Having an unfair advantage
- Seeking special favors or attention by sucking up to those in authority
- Trying to make them look bad

Those who condemn tend to be the most dangerous because they hurt feelings, reputations and the dreams of those who want to succeed. They are afraid of, and feel threatened by, those who pursue excellence. They have decided that they cannot compete so they want to discourage those who seek greatness. Condemnation is sometimes a cry for help. They do not want to be alone in their mediocrity and will try to keep you down with them. As we discussed in a previous chapter, on your journey to reaching your dreams, there are inevitable changes that you will need to make in your life. Distancing yourself from condemners will be one of those critical changes that you will need to make. They are toxic people who will only poison your environment.

– Conform

The Merriam-Webster dictionary defines "conform" as "to be similar to or the same as something; to obey or agree with something; to do what other people do; to behave in a way that is accepted by most people."[2] In other words, to conform is to go with the flow or go along with the crowd. If the crowd is highly motivated, working toward a brighter future and positive goals, you are in good company. This group will help you to stay focused and achieve your goals. However, if the crowd is negative, one that is unmotivated and content with average performance, then conformance will have a detrimental effect on your performance.

The negative conformers are permanent followers of the wrong crowd. You will see them in the assembly of the disgruntled. Generally, those on the outside looking in will paint everyone within that group with the same brush. They will be dismissed as people who have nothing of value to offer. Since you are working so hard toward your goals and desires, you definitely do not want to be a part of this group, even by accident. You want your contributions to shine. Moreover, you want your dreams to come to fruition. Therefore, you want to do all that you can to make sure your efforts are on full display.

Rather than conforming, there will be occasions where you will be required to be a leader. This strong character trait will cause your associates to imitate you and conform to you as a standard of excellence. You have a brain and free will, choose wisely and follow what is good and constructive. You can teach people how to compete instead of conforming to the whims of negative people.

– Confuse

A company that cannot compete against a worthy opponent will try to use their power to confuse the consumer. A company may disseminate false information about a competitor's product. This misinformation could suggest that the product underperforms or it could call into question the integrity of anyone selling the product. Their goal is to plant seeds of doubt in the mind of someone who has to decide between itself and its competitor. They may even go so far as to provide the competing company with misinformation, to obfuscate their actual intentions. While someone may rightfully question whether this is an ethical strategy, it is a commonly known and employed business tactic.

As a student of the game, you must be fully aware that someone may use these tactics against you. In the workplace, someone seeking the same promotion as you are may attempt to impugn your character or mischaracterize your accomplishments. In an academic setting, other students may hijack the lesson plan and decrease the level of information taught in the classroom. In both the work and academic setting, the confusion often comes from someone who is attempting to divert attention from their own shortcomings or mistakes.

The Competition Strikes Back

We earlier discussed the value in preparing for the competition. Remember, the competition is also preparing for you. They are involved in similar research and game planning. Additionally, your competition may not be sitting next to you in the classroom or live in your community. They may be thousands of miles and several countries and continents away. Their motivations are myriad. Some want to escape poverty while some may have dreams of market domination. Others, still, may be searching for opportunities that they believe only exist in certain regions of the world. This hunger for success will drive them and cause them to sacrifice and postpone pleasures for a more lasting satisfaction.

Are you ready to meet that level of competition head on? You may not be able to witness the preparation of your competitors, but you have to assume they have the same passions as you. Larry Bird, a professional basketball player and Hall of Fame inductee began practicing as a small child. In his back yard, in a small town in Indiana, he would shoot the basketball eight to ten hours a day. He said he went to bed each night wondering if someone anywhere else in the world practiced harder and longer.[3]

How do you think the competition prepares for you?

- Would they be worried, intimidated or complacent?
- Would they lose sleep if they knew you were their opponent?
- Would the thought of your preparation, determination, hard work and skills cause them to doubt themselves?
- Are they a student of the game?

Competition will not go away. It is everywhere. You compete for the interest of potential life partners, for a spot in an elite school and for the job you desire. Even with your dream house, you may find yourself in a bidding war with another interested buyer. Some people make the mistake of not taking the competition seriously. Companies are looking for a competitive advantage. You should do the same. You should plan for the competition because they are planning for you. Understanding the dynamics of competition increases your effectiveness, as you unlock your leadership greatness.

Building Your Network

"It is not what you know, but who you know." You may have heard this phrase or a variation over the years. Of course, you actually do have to know something. What this phrase really means is that successful people need others to help them make it in this world. They cannot make it on their work alone. A student of the game is aware of this fact.

All successful people need someone to help them reach their goal. Both George Fraser and James Malinchak talk about the effectiveness of networking. They mentioned that the focus of your networking conversations should be what you can do for the people you meet. This is not the opportunity to dominate the conversation with personal stories or to get them to do something for you. James even coined a phrase that says, "When you meet someone new, they don't want to learn about you."[4]

Establishing a network of relationships will be a key factor in your future success. You will reap great rewards if you have a network that is sizable and diverse. You want your circle of contacts to include people with different skills and experiences. When assessing the quality of your network, ask yourself:

1. Who do I know?
2. Who knows me?
3. What do they think of me?
4. What can they do for me?
5. What will they do for me?

Who Do You Know?

It today's competitive environment, it is critical to know a lot of people and the right people. If you struggle with physics, you want to talk to someone who is good in physics. It will be to your advantage to have a large number of contacts who can come to your aid and provide advice, references, resources and recommendations. Your college professors are noted authorities in their areas of expertise. Make sure you get to know them and understand their contributions to their fields of study. Similarly, if you are also currently in the workforce, it would serve you well to get to know those throughout the organization who have expertise in areas you would like to explore. I firmly believe that somebody knows somebody who I need to know. The same is true for you. A warm greeting and a respectful acknowledgement are often the beginning gestures of unlocking hidden opportunities. You should be courteous and respectful because you are supposed to be courteous and respectful. However, the benefits of this admirable behavior, while not the driver of your behavior, could be substantial and invaluable down the road.

Who Knows You?

During your academic years, you will encounter fellow students and professors, and will have varying degrees of interactions with them. In many cases, these very people will potentially have useful information or contacts that may lead to opportunities in the future. They may have particular insight into the graduate program or career field that you want to enter. They may be one of the many professors who serves as a consultant and has contacts with major corporations and small businesses. They may have grown up in a country to which you would like to relocate. They may be someone who is particularly socially adept and your association with them may introduce you to a wider social circle. For these reasons, it will be to your advantage to cultivate these relationships. Be open, move around and meet people who have diverse interests and backgrounds. Do not hesitate to seek an introduction to someone you find especially interesting. While some may consider this move to be political or "sucking up," it is an invaluable way to expand your network. It also gives you an opportunity to make a positive impression on a wider group of people. The foundation of the strategy is to engage in activities, reach out and make connections, so people are aware of you. You can execute this strategy in an academic or athletic setting or through volunteer work on campus or in the community.

What Do They Think of You?

This is an important question, the answer to which may vary depending on who you ask. It is easy for one person to interpret "reserved and thoughtful" as "aloof and judgmental." On the other hand, "outgoing and outspoken" can be read as "brash and overly opinionated." The reality may lie anywhere along the spectrum. It is up to you to determine the prevailing perception of you. Consider asking your close friends and acquaintances to give you feedback on how you interact with others. Also, consider speaking with your professors to determine whether your actions represent that of an attentive, engaged and intellectually curious student. You may find that people view you exactly the way in which you would like them to perceive you. However, you may get a wake-up call. You do not want the right people to have the wrong impression of you. Character and integrity are valuable assets for school, your professional life and leadership positions. Your reputation will be the difference between prosperity and missing opportunities. Be open to constructive feedback and be prepared to make necessary changes.

What Can They Do for You?

It is obvious what some people can do for you. They can introduce you to influential people. They can assist with research projects. Your professors can provide referrals to help you land a job or a spot in a postgraduate program. A part-time employer can serve as a reference as you seek to move into a full time position in your career of choice. Social networks of friends and acquaintances may grant you contacts that may benefit you someday.

Still others may be able to help you in ways that may not be as obvious. You may not know the value or connections of people you meet. Some people are surprised to learn that a person in a low-level position may have connections to very influential power brokers. Do not make the mistake of underestimating someone's power and influence. This mistake could have a detrimental effect and you may never know it. Consider a very common scenario that occurs in pharmaceutical sales. A sales representative goes into a doctor's office with the desire to make a pitch to the doctor. He encounters the office manager and makes his request for a visit in a less than cordial manner. Unwisely, he has dismissed the office manager as a low-level employee. Many times that person turns out to be the doctor's family member, often a spouse. The sales representative finds out later, when it is too late, that his actions prevented him from seeing the doctor. The lesson here is that you may not know whether someone is in a position to help or hinder you. Therefore, it is wise to treat everyone with respect and to recognize that everyone has something of value to offer.

What Will They Do for You?

Just because somebody can do something for you does not mean that they will. You have to be someone that they want to help. Your character and work ethic will distinguish you from others. When people admire you and have faith in your abilities, they are more inclined to help you. Further, if you have shown yourself to be willing to help others, they may want to return the favor. Others may want to be connected with the career of a winner or a rising star. They may provide you with assistance because they know that one day you may be in position to further their own goals.

Another way to determine what someone will do for you may be based on what they have done for you in the past. If they have a history of being helpful to you or others, they have already proven they want you to succeed. Do not abuse their assistance, but do not forget about them either.

The type of assistance that you will need on your path to leadership greatness likely will not fall into your lap. Nor should you expect it to. In the scenarios discussed above, you will most likely need to be the initiator. Some people may not know you need help, may be preoccupied with other matters or they may want you to ask for it to see how badly you are committed to your goal. Do not be afraid to ask for help if you need it. As stated earlier, everyone needs help sometimes. When you ask for assistance, whether it is for guidance, a recommendation or an introduction, be sure to demonstrate that you are willing to return the favor in whatever way you ethically can. This offer will place them in a better mood to help you. You will have shown that you are not selfish and that you appreciate the assistance they are providing.

Six Personalities on the Path to Progress

You will encounter diversity along the path to progress. There is a variety of personalities on your journey. Some are willing to assist you, while others may be an impediment to your achievement. Six profiles are highlighted here based on my observations of individuals and group interactions. They are the relaters, waiters, haters, traitors, debaters and spectators. No one is exclusively one profile all the time. In addition, you may find that you need to have specific personalities in your corner to achieve a specific goal. It is important to identify these personalities in order to enlist their assistance or to avoid their negative attacks on your well-being and your ability to achieve outstanding results.

Relaters

These individuals relate to your dreams, goals and aspirations. They are in accord with your mission to succeed. There is a connection, commitment and compatibility with your dream. They relate positively to your intentions and seek the best for you. They are on sometimes on the sidelines or in the game with you as supporters, cheerleaders and advocates. It warms your heart to look in your corner and see the relaters who want you to make it.

Waiters

Waiters and waitresses have a servant's heart. They are not individuals hired by you, but people who voluntarily serve you on your journey. They are your friends, parents, teachers, coaches, mentors and positive peers. They may be anonymous or strangers who say a kind word or perform a good deed. These individuals derive satisfaction from being of service to, and being a part of the delegation responsible for, your achievements.

I ran the Chicago Marathon twice and each time I received an extra boost from the crowd of supporters who lined the streets, raising signs of encouragement and cheering us on. They screamed out the numbers of the runners and some of them provided us with water, snacks and other services. Their only goal was to make our grueling journey a little better. You may recall a waiter or waitress who gave you outstanding service. They asked all of the right questions in order to serve you better. They went out of their way to make your visit an enjoyable and memorable experience.

Haters

You may have encountered these individuals. They are outwardly against you. They may be jealous, insecure or just plain malicious in their attitude towards you. We will discuss them further in the next chapter under people who act with malicious intent to harm others. You may not have done anything against these people, but they see you and immediately resent you and your accomplishments. Haters are committed to bringing you down. They celebrate and laugh when you stumble. They have the resentment to match your contentment and find great satisfaction whenever you experience difficulties. Haters are prone to go to great lengths to place barriers in front of you and to turn people against you. They are constantly questioning your motives, while developing conspiracy theories to discredit your work.

Haters are very dangerous because of their capacity to spread malicious lies and rumors while attacking your reputation. Their outward expression of contempt may not be to your face, but many people will be exposed to their feelings.

Traitors

Traitors may get very close to you and win your confidence. You may trust them only to find out that they were false friends. They will work quietly to unravel and discredit your progress to success. They will secretly try to undermine your efforts and tell people about your innermost secrets and weaknesses. Traitors may start out as relaters, but somewhere along the way, they turn against you. Hopefully you will find out soon enough that they cannot be trusted. They are backbiters and back stabbers. They may be passive-aggressive, sneaky and secretive. Traitors may ruin your reputation by selling your secrets to the highest bidder.

Because others believe that the traitors are your friends, the traitors' words ring with truth and credibility to an unsuspecting audience. Traitors will break your heart because of their proximity to your inner circle. They are on the inside and privy to your thoughts, feelings and actions. It is important to develop the skill in neutralizing the harmful effects that this particular personality type can place on your path to progress.

Debaters

While you are committed to your journey, you will find a number of people challenging you every step of the way. They try to talk you out of success. They will question your sacrifice and try to discourage you from "wasting your time." They will give you countless counter arguments and examples of others who failed through no fault of their own. They will persistently challenge the value of your dreams and the foolishness of your work ethic. Debaters will make you question your intelligence and qualifications for your objectives.

Debaters, however, can strengthen your resolve and survival skills. When you successfully counter their arguments, you will be stronger against other opponents. They actually prepare you for meaningful discourse with the conscientious objectors who are against your desire to be successful.

Spectators

In many respects, your journey to succeed is a competitive event. There are spectators who are alongside the roadway. Other spectators are in the stands watching the game. They do not get involved in the activities. They may cheer, but the cheers may not be for you. You may see the spectators in the stands, but you do not know their allegiance. You just know that they are present. They do not personally give you words of encouragement, as is the case with relaters and the waiters. You may not know if they are against you like the haters, debaters and the traitors.

Haters and traitors are potentially destructive. You need to find out who they are and develop strategies, structures and individuals to shield you from their insecurities. Haters and traitors attack you from different positions. Haters are outwardly against you. Traitors are inwardly against you. They gained your confidence and many times, you were unaware of their insidious nature.

Some debaters are convinced they are trying to protect you by talking you out of your dream. They may feel the dream is too dangerous and you may be hurt and they want to spare you the grief and humiliation associated with failing. However, many debaters are insecure and do not want you to succeed because they will take it personally. If you succeed and they do not, they will see themselves as failures.

The spectators may be harmless, but they should be more than a witness along your path to progress. Spectators should get involved in the game and become relaters and waiters to support your cause. It is wonderful when spectators decide to be a part of the success of others. This service to others could be a major personal development growth opportunity on their path to becoming a leader.

These six personalities are present any time you try to accomplish something. When you unlock your leadership greatness, which includes the ability to work with and benefit from a diverse group of personalities, you will improve your chances for success. You will be conscious of the styles that fit your personality. You will also recognize the personalities in others and develop a strategy to utilize the information to your advantage.

6 Personalities on the Path to Progress

- **Relaters**
  - Relate to your dreams, goals and aspirations
  - In sync with you, can feel you and are in your corner
  - Supporters, cheerleaders and advocates
- **Waiters / Waitresses**
  - They serve you and improve the quality of your journey
  - Satisfied when you are happy and love to positively contribute to your growth
  - Friends, parents, coaches, mentors, positive peers and helpful strangers
- **Haters**
  - Outwardly against you
  - Want you to fail and may actively contribute to your fall
  - Jealous, insecure or feel threatened by your presence
  - They take your success personally

- **Traitors**
  - Inwardly against you
  - People on your side who secretly betray your trust
  - Spread your secrets for selfish motives as they violate your confidence
- **Debaters**
  - They try to talk you out of your dreams with a point by point rebuttal
  - Challenge and question your desire to succeed by making you feel foolish
  - They are your greatest critics, yet they can prepare you for other detractors
- **Spectators**
  - Non committal, but always present in the stands as witnesses
  - No personal words of encouragement to show they are on your side
  - Unsure of their allegiance because of their lack of commitment

Watchwell
Communications, Inc.

Discussion Topics for Personal Reflection or Small Groups

1. Which of the six components of the competitive response module (compete, concede, complain, condemn, conform and confuse) applies to you? Do you know people who fit under each category?

2. Do you have a group of advisors that you consult on specific issues?

3. Do you have a mentor or coach?

4. It is important to know people who have power. Whether your acquaintance wit those people will lead to real rewards is dependent on other factors. There are five components:

    a. Who do you know?

    b. Who knows you?

    c. What do they think of you?

    d. What can they do for you?

    e. What will they do for you?

    Analyze your current situation in light of these five questions. Is your network strong?

5. Discuss the six personalities on the path to progress and identify the one that is your greatest threat. Identify people who are your greatest supporters and how they have demonstrated their support.

CHAPTER 4

MASTER THE FUNDAMENTALS

Master the basics through practice and mental rehearsal

"I was influenced when I was younger by the cartoon movies that Disney put out, like Cinderella and what not. I watched those movies over and over when I was younger and the music is ingrained into my head. Nowadays, I'm still humming the tunes. It taught me the fundamentals."

—Zac Efron

"Fundamentals are the building blocks of fun."

—Mikhail Baryshnikov

"Pressure is a privilege."

—Billie Jean King

Your GPA is like your GPS - it tells you where you are and where you're going.

Judgment

In my years in business, periodically the leadership team determined that our employees had strayed from the fundamentals. Soon thereafter, management would initiate a "back to the basics" campaign. When something goes wrong, usually you will find that you will need to make minor adjustments to your techniques to get back on the right track.

It is critical for you to fortify the fundamentals, especially now while you are in your academic years. You will set the foundation for building your career credentials. Using your judgment to make the most informed decisions will be one of the keys to your success. Being able to make an informed decision comes only after you have done significant information gathering. Therefore, a crucial part of mastering this fundamental is the need to ask questions and identifying the best available sources for answers. All of the decisions that you make, and the judgment required to make the right decision, will depend on the quality of the information that you gather.

In business, there is a peculiar phenomenon. People will not seek out help when they first recognize that they need it. Their boss or others may say, "Let me know if there is a problem." Despite this standing offer of assistance, way too often the panicked employee will call at the last possible opportunity. As they tell of their "dilemma," you can almost hear "glug, glug, glug," as if they are talking while their head is under water. They did not call until the water level was nearly over their head. Why did they wait? Their responses would usually include a variation of these explanations:

1. They did not want to disturb the leader because they knew they were busy

2. They thought they could make it on their own

3. They were embarrassed

4. They did not want to admit they needed help

Students also make the mistake of not reaching out to their professors or tutors until it is almost too late. Professors may have large class sizes and busy schedules, but they are there to help students succeed. Professors are like many leaders. They will not care more about your success than you do. At the same time, they are eager to help those who want to succeed. Seek them out early, gather much needed information and strengthen your ability to synthesize data for future decision-making.

Self-Motivation for Excellence

Self-motivation is a fundamental skill that everyone should have. Self-motivation involves maintaining a laser focus on the goals that you have set for yourself and tending to the individual steps toward those goals so that you remain on track. In Chapter 2, I discussed the types of steps you can take on a daily basis to ensure that you remain focused on your dreams (i.e., daily affirmations, journaling, regularly meeting with a mentor). These are all integral parts of the fundamentals of self-motivation. In addition, recognize the importance of proper thinking to help you take your performance to a higher level and differentiate yourself from others.

I have learned that the way you mentally frame the events in your life will determine your actions and success. You must realize that appropriate thinking can lead to appropriate actions. Additionally, it is important to be optimistic. Dr. Martin Seligman, in his book Learned Optimism, said, "Optimistic individuals produce more, particularly under pressure, than do pessimists." Moreover, he states, "What is crucial is what you think when you fail, using the power of 'non-negative thinking.' Changing the destructive things you say to yourself when you experience the setbacks that life deals all of us is the central skill of optimism."[1]

In his timeless recording, The Strangest Secret, Earl Nightingale defined success as "the progressive realization of a worthy goal or ideal." Mr. Nightingale also noted "You are now, and you do become, what you think about."[2] We can influence our level of success by altering our thinking. Many experts claim that we only use 10% of our mental ability, so therefore there is plenty of room for growth into your virtually untapped reserves.

William James said, "The greatest discovery of our generation is that human beings can alter their lives by altering their attitudes of mind."[3] George Bernard Shaw wrote, "People are always blaming their circumstances for what they are. I don't believe in circumstances. The people who get on in this world are the people who look for the circumstances they want and if they can't find them, make them."[4] Success, therefore, is primarily mental. Motivation is mental. The desire to succeed is mental. You can achieve your goals if you control your thinking. Since one of your goals is to unlock your leadership greatness, it begins with proper thinking. Motivation is fundamental.

Time Management and Timing

How you use the time given to you is your choice. How you manage your time will contribute to or take away from your ability to be successful. People may be smarter, stronger or have more money and resources, but you can achieve your goals and minimize the impact of their advantages by using your time wisely. Part of your strategy should be to think more than others think on the critical issues. This involves directing your thoughts to solve problems, answer questions and develop ideas. One of my favorite phrases is "someone may be smarter than me, but chances are, I am thinking more than they are. I am always thinking, using my time to make up for any difference in intellect, resources and privileges."[5]

According to Dr. Phillip Zimbardo, by the time he is 21 years old, the average young man will have spent 10,000 hours playing video games.[6] Many of these 10,000 hours are spent alone, which in turn leads to many missed opportunities to develop social skills. In his book, Outliers, Malcolm Gladwell reviewed the research on select successful people. He examined the Beatles during their time in Liverpool, Steve Jobs from Apple Computer, a chess master and experts from many fields. He wanted to determine the amount of practice time, study time or performance time it took to become an expert in the defined area. He found out that the amount of time required to be an expert was 10,000 hours. This is approximately three hours a day, seven days a week and fifty weeks a year, for 10 years.[7]

In one of my speaking engagements with a group of young students, I discussed the Gladwell findings. When I asked my students whether they would like to spend 10,000 hours to be an expert in a particular field or to get into multiple chambers in a video game, they were undecided. Understandably, it is hard for preteens to wrap their minds around spending ten years to work on a future goal. You, on the other hand, are at a time in your life where you are poised to embark on the career of your choice. Now is the time to consider the appropriate value and use of their time.

Time Management with the Know System™

It is important for you to manage your time, which means you must learn to manage yourself. Managing yourself will require you to make decisions based on what is most important to you personally and professionally. The Know System is a decision-making tool. In Chapter 7, I will discuss the greater applicability of The Know System. For now, I would like to discuss how this tool can be used in the context of time management. The Know System relies on exploration of other words that are formed from the letters in the word "KNOW." The key words are WON, OWN, KNOW, NOW, NO, ON and WOK.

First, you begin with "WON," as in the concept of winning. This is your goal, dream or objective. What does it mean for you to say you have won? As we stated earlier, everyone likes to win. What does success look like to you? What are your goals and priorities? These will determine the things that are important to you and on which you will spend the bulk of your time. Your decisions should work around your goals and help you to reach them.

Second, you have to "OWN" the responsibility of managing your time. It will not manage itself. You have to take to control of your schedule and ensure that activities are in line with your goals.

Third, you have to "KNOW" yourself and the challenges that will enhance or distract you on the road to success. You may find that during certain times of the day you are more easily distracted. In addition, there may be people who often interrupt you when you are trying to complete an assignment. You have to know and identify roadblocks and barriers and create a strategy to prevent them from affecting your work. For example, you may share your schedule with friends and family so that they know which times you will be unavailable for impromptu chat sessions. Also, if your mind tends to wander in the late afternoon, consider scheduling your daily workouts during this time.

Fourth, you must evaluate what you are doing "NOW." Are your current actions in line with your goals? Are your current actions moving you closer to your objectives? If the answer to either question is "no," you must reassess your priorities. Time management expert Alan Laken, in his book How to get Control of Your Time and Your Life, suggests that you should rank your goals and actions as A's, B's or C's. The A's are the most important. The B's are next in importance and C's, while important, are lowest in priority. He encourages you to make a daily "To Do" list of the tasks you need to perform, again arranged according to A's, B's and C's.[8] This level of active prioritizing ensures that you are spending your time on the goals that will have the higher payoff. The "To Do" list will influence what you are doing NOW and keep you steadily moving toward your goals.

The fifth key word in the Know System is "NO." There are times when you must say "no" to something or someone who is not a priority. You may have to work on a project or study for an exam, only to have your friends pressuring you to "hang out" with them. You cannot be all things to all people. Nor can you do everything people want you to do. This will lead to burnout and a disorganized schedule. You may have to say "no" to yourself if your thoughts and actions are out of focus. While it may not be easy to say "no" to some people or even to yourself, you must have the will to do so. Tempting distractions will cause you to take longer to finish assignments, miss deadlines, lose sleep and may affect your grades and results. There are people or activities that are time bandits or time wasters. You should determine who or what they are and eliminate them.

The sixth word, "ON," dictates that you must be "ON" at all times. You must be dedicated to, and energized by, the work you have to do. If you let down your guard, you may find those time bandits we discussed above slowly eating into your valuable time and shifting your focus from your goals. Guard your time closely and wisely. It is an extremely valuable asset.

Our final word is "WOK." Sometimes you have to stir things up a bit, similar to when cooking a stir-fry meal in a wok. If you have done something a certain way and it no longer works for you, you have to make a change. If you have done something a certain way and someone has a better way of doing, you must be open to change. It is important to be versatile and flexible if it allows you to manage your time better. You may feel as if you already have a good handle on your time management, but there is always room for growth. There is a common saying, "if it ain't broke, don't fix it." Robert J. Kriegel has a different view of this concept. His book, "If it Ain't Broke. . .Break It!"[9] challenges you to think of ways to improve everything. Breaking, mixing or stirring things up also shows the importance of innovation through new ideas and new techniques.

Using Your Time Wisely

With a full schedule, which may include school and work, you may find yourself with very little time to work on your goals. You have day-to-day obligations, such as completing coursework, participating in student organizations or working part-time. While these activities are necessary in the big picture of reaching your goals, they may leave you feeling as if there is no time for anything else. A key question to ask yourself is "How can I use my time better?"

People spend time:

- Riding public transportation
- Walking long distances for work or exercise
- Waiting in lines
- Working on things that do not require a lot of thinking
- Sitting in class or meetings when there is down time

What are you thinking about during these times? You can use this time to concentrate on the key areas around your schooling and career. You can mentally rehearse for an upcoming presentation. You can train your mind to work on solving problems. A trained mind can come up with the solution to a problem while you are working on something unrelated to the problem. Remember always to have a notepad or other device handy so that you can jot down your ideas.

As the world becomes more and more competitive, it is imperative that you use your time in the most productive manner. Make the most of your time, no matter how small the block of time may seem. Competition is everywhere and everyone else is learning more and studying harder to succeed. You must do the same.

Understand the Value of Your Time

Some people place a value on their time to help them devote their time to the most important things. If you have a profession, you know how much you are paid per hour and you can use that hourly rate as a proxy for the value of the time you spend on other activities. For example, assume you have a job that pays $200 an hour. Someone asks you to spend your time on a different task, which would require that you forego working on your regular job. It may be for less money or no money at all. You must then compare this other activity to the value of your time. Does the activity provide a benefit so great that you would be willing to pass on the higher compensation of your regular job? Will you be able to acquire some much-needed skill that you may not be able to obtain otherwise? Will the activity bring you an intangible satisfaction that is not quantifiable by money? If the answers to these questions is "no," then you may wish to pass on this other opportunity.

If you are in school you may not have a dollar figure to place on activities, but you can still rank them based on the priorities you have in life. If you feel your family and friends are A's, if something comes along that is a C you would not let them replace your family time. If your studies are an A and friends come along you may list your friends as an A as well and you must decide which one will get your time. If you have several A's, rank them as A1, A2, and A3 to help decide which A is more important at a given time. Of course, the priority ranking will undoubtedly shift given the circumstances. This is to be expected and is not a problem. What is most important is that you maintain proper focus and balance the priorities in your life to keep you moving in the direction of your goals.

Above, I indicated that an activity might bring you intangible satisfaction that is not easily quantifiable. One such example is a hobby. How much time do you spend on hobbies? As you consider how to prioritize your time, consider this: many businesses are built on skills and interests developed as a hobby. Over time, many people find that hobbies can be an excellent foundation upon which to build a business. They often began their hobby as a form of recreation and a way to explore a subject with which they were fascinated. They may have spent hundreds of unpaid hours pursuing an interest but ultimately they were able to turn their time investment into research and development for a potential business venture. A hobby rarely provides you with a monetary benefit. Indeed, it may even cost you money. However, the potential exists to learn new skills, reduce stress and provide a foundation for ideas for a business venture down the road. A hobby is therefore fruitful on many levels and is worth the time invested.

Timing

You have heard it said or even said it yourself, "Timing is everything." There are times in life when you must synchronize your watch in order to do something at the right moment. You are aware of the value of excellent timing. People wait outside sporting venues and department stores to be the first in line to get a soon to be sold out ticket or the best items on sale. We praise public speakers and comedians for their gift of excellent timing. You probably have someone in your life who has a knack for knowing just the right time to deliver some much needed comfort. The value of timing is emphasized in advertising. Paul Masson, a brand of wine, had an advertising slogan that said, "We will sell no wine before its time." Similarly, an investor knows that a properly timed "buy or sell" decision could result in a major profit. The ability to execute something at the right time is an asset and an amazing talent.

Timing plays a major role in self-discipline. We learn that to achieve greatness we need to sacrifice. The word sacrifice means to deprive oneself, to give up something of value or to forego some benefit or pleasure. Alternatively, you can view sacrifice as postponing, reprioritizing or placing something on a different schedule. I do not want you to think only in terms of denying yourself, but of changing the timing of your actions and activities. If your friends want you to go out for a movie when you should be studying, you should question, "Is this the right time?" You do not have to deprive yourself of fun, friendship or happy moments, but you may have to reschedule to a more appropriate time.

You may need only to alter the timing. You may have to operate on a different clock than your friends, but you are not avoiding them or denying yourself, but moving the activity to a time where it is more consistent with your dreams and goals. Be in control of your time. You may decide to spend time with them at a later, more reasonable hour. If you wait until later to study or get your life together, you might miss the opportunity to prepare for a career.

Many of the choices and decisions you make in life are right or wrong based on when you make them. When trying to determine if the timing is ideal, consider the following factors:

- Are the right resources present? Resources include people, money, tools and information.

- Are you at the right maturity level for the situation, i.e., are you emotionally, physically, mentally, financially and spiritually prepared for the challenge?

If you gain better control and improve your sense of timing, you will be in a position to lead a more productive and satisfying life. If you move activities around and slot them in better locations, you can accomplish the priorities of your life and reach your goals. This may mean postponing some actions until later. You should not view this as a form of sacrifice or deprivation. You are using timing, as would a great public speaker, surgeon, musician, businessperson or comedian, to perform the right action at the appropriate time. By making sure all the key elements are in line, you are assuring the most desired outcome.

Communication Skills

Communication skills are key to a leader's effectiveness. This fundamental skill, when mastered, will give you an edge on your competitors. Individuals with the strongest presentation skills are often the first to be considered for the lead on key assignments. Those with the most effective communications skills will often be the voice for the entire group, whether it is a business committee or student group. Not only will your communication skills lead to greater visibility, but it will also allow you more opportunities to hone your skill in a variety of settings.

Communication skill involves both language mastery and situational awareness. The language mastery will come, in part, with your command of the written and spoken word. The skill you develop writing reports in college will benefit you throughout your life. It will prepare you for many occasions where you will be required to present a concise, persuasive report. This may be a business proposal, a book idea or a marketing pitch. More immediately, it may be a cover letter for an entry-level job. No matter the opportunity, your ability to draw in the reader will be a critical skill. A significant part of developing this skill comes from your general level of knowledge. You may have heard the phrase: "leaders are readers." This phrase speaks to the notion that a great leader has a quest for knowledge and a desire to strive continuously for greatness. The more you read and expand your knowledge base, the better your ability to communicate with, and influence, a broader range of people. Furthermore, you will be able to provide greater value to those you lead because the knowledge you acquire through reading will afford you a broader perspective to address their questions and problems.

The ability to be a great speaker comes with practice and a good deal of courage. There are those among us that have a natural talent for speaking confidently in front of others. No matter your comfort level, it is imperative that you take every opportunity to hone your ability to speak in front of an audience. You should look for opportunities to gain speaking experience. It is a good idea to start small and work your way up. I have seen people stand when they ask a question to get accustomed to speaking in front of a small group. Several venues can serve as a training ground for speaking. Consider the following:

- speak before your fraternity/sorority or dormitory council meetings

- volunteer for a leadership position where you have to provide reports or updates to the group
- join Toastmasters, an excellent organization that focuses on training confident public speakers
- take a speech class as one of your electives in college
- volunteer at a local school where you speak to students about preparing for success
- become a mentor to small groups
- volunteer at your place of worship and search for leadership and speaking opportunities

The ability to read people, through understanding body language, is as important as reading books or other materials. This is part of the skill of situational awareness that I mentioned above. There is a body of evidence around understanding people's nonverbal cues that can help you understand the messages people are sending to you more completely.[10] You may notice leaning in to the speaker (a sign of interest) or lack of eye contact (a sign of distraction). When you understand these cues fully, you may need to adjust your intended message. This understanding will allow you to tailor your message for the particular audience, be it an audience of one or one hundred. Understanding the many factors that can influence whether your speech will be well received is critical. For example, if your audience is comprised of members who are highly knowledgeable about your subject matter, you may want to avoid a speech that is too elementary in nature.

Listen and Learn

Cocky & Rhodette

by Orlando Ceaser

They never said, "I told you so" with their lips, but I could see it in their eyes.

I told a group of students a story about the road. There was a man who walked ahead of everyone. He was a trailblazer. Some called him a scout or pioneer. After traveling a long way up the road, he noticed a number of things in the environment. He decided to draw a map and write down the experiences on his journey. The traveler saw dangers where people made bad decisions and cost them their freedom and their lives. There were corners where people were taken by surprise and ambushed. There were forks in the road that were confusing. There were potholes, sinkholes and traps of all kinds.

There were also many pleasant events, as people experienced success by obeying the rules and following the right system. After traveling for a while, he turned around to retrace his steps. He wanted to share his journey with the people he met along the path. He wanted others to know about the dangers, traps and potholes that they should avoid. When he approaches you, would you want to hear the stories of what was waiting for you? Of course, you would want to know. That is the role that parents and elders play in your lives. Your professors, mentors and coaches have traveled the road ahead of you. They have seen the dangers, traps, potholes and areas where people were ambushed and robbed. They want you to benefit from their experience, so that you make better decisions about which fork in the road to take. You must listen and learn from the messages.

Some things you want to learn for yourself. Indeed, some lessons will only resonate if you have firsthand experience. As an adult, you will want to explore relationships, careers, hobbies and other adventures. Go for it. Remember, however, the wisdom of those who have had the same experiences. Like a true leader, you will forge your own path. As an exceptional leader, you will gather tools along the way and some of the greatest tools will be the wisdom gained from the trailblazers.

Leadership Greatness in Interviewing

Most people think of an interview as an event where a candidate sits down in front of one or more people to pitch their qualifications. I want you to think of an interview as much more than a single event. I want you to think of an interview as a process or a journey. Every interaction is an interview, an opportunity to express your skills and abilities. Every day you are preparing for your first or your next interview. When you adopt this mindset and act accordingly, you may impress people who in turn may offer you, or recommend you for, an assignment at a later date.

You should also think of an interview as something that is in the STARS for you. You should view your interaction, your interview as:

S = Story
T = Telling
A = About
R = Results

It is an opportunity to share stories about your accomplishments. Depending upon the job, company or individual for which you are interviewing, you will know on which achievements to place the greater emphasis. Later, I will discuss other STARS to bear in mind around preparing your responses to interview questions.

You should also approach your interview as something important enough to require thought and preparation. A way to prepare mentally for the interview is by evaluating the word PREP.

P = Plan
R = Research
E = Examine
P = Practice

PREP is a necessary process to ensure that you will address key areas before the interview session. PREP will ensure that you are ready.

Plan

You should target the kind of job that you want to pursue. You should develop a written strategy and become familiar with all of its details. Your plans should be comprised of industries, companies and specific job assignments that match your skills and qualifications. Planning should also include the actual interview and potential responses to key questions.

Research

Investigate the companies through their websites, employees, customers and any material available on the Internet and within the public domain. Most companies expect that you will have a working knowledge of their organization prior to the interview. This demonstrates your initiative and hunger for the position. This necessary step meets their minimum expectations.

Research yourself and your files. Do you have data to support your claims, accomplishments and accolades? This may include certificates, letters of recognition, recommendations and awards. Choose three or four areas that you can revisit in order to answer questions about your accomplishments. These areas could be jobs, class projects, volunteer assignments and hobbies. If you understand your performance in these areas, you will be able to answer questions about your accomplishments in a comfortable and confident manner.

An interview is an opportunity to talk about one of your favorite subjects; a subject with which you are particularly passionate and one where you have a unique perspective based on your personal experience. Learn and master the highlights from a few select areas to keep yourself confident and focused during the interview.

Examine

Know yourself by exploring the key areas mentioned above. Go deeper to assess your strengths, weaknesses, and areas that may cause you difficulty in an interview. Anticipate your responses to questions and prepare the responses in a favorable light.

In a mock interview that I monitored, a young man stated that he gets bored easily. His mentor asked that he rephrase his response. Although the statement may have been true, the mentor recognized that "easily bored" is not a selling point. After some thought, they arrived at alternate, more positive responses. "I like a challenging situation" and "I like to be in a busy environment, so that I can stay focused on achieving results." These new responses are as equally true as the original one; however, the focus is now on the results that would be of interest to an employer.

Practice

Practice means to role-play or physically act out the interviews. You can do this through mental rehearsals or in one-on-one sessions with peers, coaches and mentors. Another good way to practice is to use recording devices, such as a digital recorder, so that you may have visual feedback of your performance. You should practice until you can comfortably relay answers to key questions expected during the interview.

Now that you have an understanding of the fundamentals of interviewing as a mindset, I want to talk about some of the nuts and bolts of formal interviewing.

Interviewer Intent

- To hire the best candidate from a crowded field of applicants

- To hire the "right fit" which will allow the company to recoup its investment

Interviewer Philosophies (techniques)

- Good Cop, Bad Cop — A technique used where one person appears to be your friend and the other person the villain who tries to intimidate you. Candidates may say things to the Good Cop that they will regret later. The Bad Cop may cause you to be flustered and lose your composure. The objective is to see how you act under pressure.

- Search for Knock out Factors — Since the field contains many competitive applicants, some interviewers narrow the field by looking for knock out factors. Candidates in their candor may give eliminating information, thinking it may help their cause. I have seen candidates divulge information they would not have revealed to their priest. This technique may involve waiting for candidates to hang themselves with volunteered information and also using leading questions to trap the candidate.

- The Friend — They attempt to lull you into comfort by earning your trust so that you can share everything with them.

- The Waiting Game — Some will ask a question and pause after your response to see if you will continue talking. If you feel confident that you have answered the question satisfactorily, stop talking. Ask if the interviewer needs more specifics. I have seen people use this technique and later said the candidate lacked judgment and talked too much.

The key to handling each of these scenarios is to be thoroughly knowledgeable of your information and pause before delivering your response. When you receive the question, do not be swayed by the personality of the interviewer. Listen for the intent of the question and answer with the appropriate information from your background.

Interview Preparation

— *Know Yourself*

An interview is an opportunity to discuss yourself and all that you can offer. You should constantly make a personal inventory of who you are, to increase your self-awareness and your ability to communicate your performances to others. Prior to the interview, you should do the following:

Review Your Background
- Conduct a skills inventory. Select areas of strength and examples you would like to use to demonstrate your skills and experiences to a potential employer.

- Perform a personal SWOT (Strengths, Weaknesses, Opportunities and Threats) Analysis. The strengths and weaknesses apply to personal skills, knowledge, talent and areas that need improvement. The opportunities and threats relate to external factors that might affect your career in the future. For example, an opportunity could be that there is an increased demand for people with your skills. A threat may be a trend toward requiring higher levels of schooling for your field. This could have a detrimental effect on your employment status if you do not upgrade your skills. A threat could also be industry downsizing or a crowded job market. A SWOT analysis would help you better understand yourself and help in career planning, as you consider the opportunities and threats that exist or may exist in a few years.

Guidance for the Candidate in the Interview

Authenticity – Honesty is the best policy. Do not embellish or stretch the truth. Do not overstate the value of your role in any of your examples.

Do Not Lie – You will likely interview or interact with more than one person within the organization. Take it as a given that they will compare notes on your responses to look for inconsistencies. There is no mercy or second chances if they believe you lied to one of them. I have seen people blow an interview by a misstatement of fact on a trivial matter. You cannot expect a stranger to be forgiving under these circumstances. If they catch you in one lie, it may invalidate all of the truths you told. No matter the urge or the temptation, only tell the truth.

Beware the Race and Gender Trap – The tendency to think that just because someone is the same race or gender, you can let down your guard. This is a mistake. They are not your friends and you should make no assumptions. You owe them the respect of their position and you deserve the right to display your talent and experience in the proper perspective.

Beware of Entrapment and Trick Questions – Questions such as, "What is your greatest weakness?" or "Tell me about a time you bent the truth in order to make a sale?" Your response should put you in a positive light and show your fallibility as a work in progress. Your response should reflect something you are genuinely working on, but place it in a context that will not harm you or serve as a deal breaker.

The Interviewer is Not Your Psychiatrist – This is no time for true confessions. Do not disclose moral flaws or family secrets. Do not ask forgiveness for past transgressions. Simply provide the interviewer with the answers to their specific questions. One candidate told us she became an alcoholic when she was twelve years old. She was in her early thirties during the interview. She also discussed other questionable behaviors from her past. We never figured out why this came up and out, but the fact that she revealed such personal information cast serious doubts upon her judgment.

Long-Range Goals

Many interviewers will ask some variation of the question: "Where do you see yourself in 5 to 10 years?" Prepare a response that relates to your career in their company or their industry. Stating that you would like to be a manager is usually a good response, especially if you state the reasons why. One candidate I interviewed stated that what he really wanted to do was work for a year and then take time off to pursue his first love, music. Even if you feel this way, the interview is no place to utter this revelation. Most companies consider new hires as an investment. They will spend resources to train you and get you acclimated to the company culture. In turn, they are looking for a profitable return on that investment. They want someone who allows them to recoup their investment, become an engaged and productive employee and make the interviewer look like a genius for hiring them.

Responses to Interview Questions

It is important to think deeply about your responses to the interview questions. It is important to have a technique that will enable you to give the desired information in a manner that is precise, concise and with substance. Many companies train their personnel to answer questions using another "STAR," utilized by DDI (Development Dimensions International) in their interview training seminars.

The STAR response is as follows:
    S - Situation
    T - Task
    A - Action
    R - Result

They want a specific <u>situation or task</u>, the <u>action</u> you performed and the <u>result</u> or outcome from that action.[11] For example:

Version # 1
Interviewer:
"Tell me about a time when you delivered more than was expected of you?"

Candidate:

Situation / task: "Customer A ran out of one of their key items for one of their clients. Their wholesaler was out of stock and would not have the product for another day.

Action: I was able to call around to other stores and arranged to pick up the product and deliver it to Customer A as a favor from me.

Result: The customer was very satisfied and our relationship improved and I established a reputation for exceptional customer service."

You may want to explore the final STAR. Replace the word "Task" with the word "Thinking." This would enable you to give them some insight into your thinking and motives by stating why you performed the action.

    S - Situation
    T - Thinking
    A - Action
    R - Result

Version #2
Interviewer:

"Tell me about a time when you delivered more than was expected of you?"

Candidate:

Situation: "Customer A ran out of one of their key items for one of their clients. Their wholesaler was out of stock and would not have the product for another day.

Thinking: I was thinking that the customer might lose a client if they did not fill this order. It was also most important for the client to get their medicine and my role is to help them meet their needs.

Action: I called around to other stores and arranged to pick up the product and deliver it to the store. My relationship with the other store made this possible since they owed me a favor.

Result: Customer A was very satisfied, our relationship improved and I established a reputation for exceptional customer service."

This is an excellent way to organize your responses to ensure concise answers and avoid being wordy. If you are unsure about the depth and length of your response, ask the interviewer if he or she needs more information.

One company uses an approach, similar to the STAR but with one difference. Instead of T for task, they use O for obstacle.

S – Situation
O – Obstacle you had to overcome
A – Action performed
R – Result achieved[12]

Version #3
Interviewer:

"Tell me about a time when you delivered more than was expected of you?"

Candidate:
Situation: "Customer A ran out of one of their key items for one of their clients. There wholesaler was out of stock and would not have the product for another day.

Obstacle: The customer did not have a purchasing relationship with the other wholesalers in the area since they were a small retailer. Contacting another wholesaler was not an option.

Action: I was able to call around to other stores and arranged to pick up the product and deliver to Customer A as a favor from me.

Result: The customer was very satisfied, our relationship improved and I established a reputation for exceptional customer service."

Deliver responses that show you are a team player, but also outline clearly your role on the team to achieve the results. On any team, everyone has a role to perform that helps the team achieve its overall objective. You may say "we delivered' on our objectives, but blend in a few "I performed" this task to help the group. Remember that anything you say in an interview is subject to rebuttal and a follow-up question. Additionally you should always be prepared to go deeper in your responses if questioned

Post Interview Questions
The interviewer will give you the opportunity to ask questions.

Prepare questions from your research of the company. This shows your initiative and desire for the job.

Develop a question or two that came to mind during the interview. This shows you were paying attention. It is OK to write down their responses. You may want to ask if it is OK to write down their responses to be sure.

If you ask a question, be prepared to live with the answer. You may hear something you did not expect to hear.

Format for Interview Simulations

- Ask questions, stop, discuss and diagram each response.

- Suggest ways to improve the delivery, depth or quality of the example.

- Replay or Repeat the questions with suggested changes.

- Continue until comfortable.

You can unlock your leadership greatness and put it on full display during very effective interviews.

Discussion Topics for Personal Reflection or Small Groups

1. What are the A, B, and C priorities in your life? Rank them A1, A2, B1, B2, C1 and C2, etc.

2. How much time do you spend daily watching television, playing videogames, surfing the Internet, practicing a musical instrument or other recreational activities?

3. How much time is set aside for hobbies and recreational activities?

4. How much time do you spend reading something that is unrelated to school or work assignments?

5. The average person spends 45 to 60 minutes a day waiting for something or on someone. Describe how you use your time during these situations.

6. What are your time wasters and how are you handling them?

7. What are three of the hardest questions someone could ask you in an interview? What would be your responses to these questions?

CHAPTER 5

SET HIGH STANDARDS

Work hard to beat your personal bests and create higher goals

"Your work is going to fill a large part of life, and the only way to be truly satisfied is to do what you believe is great work. And the only way to do great work is to love what you do. If you haven't found it yet, keep looking. Don't settle. As with all matters of the heart, you'll know when you find it. And, like any great relationship, it just gets better and better as the years roll on. So keep looking, don't settle."

—Steve Jobs

"There are people who have it the same as you or worse than you, who are performing better than you. Why are you allowing this to happen? What is your reason for not giving your best?"

—Orlando Ceaser

"Today, I will do what others won't, so tomorrow I can accomplish what others can't."

—Jerry Rice

Cocky & Rhodette by Orlando Ceaser

What if your life were monitored
for quality purposes?

Values

What is important to you? Who are the people, places and things in your life that have the highest priority? What are your values, beliefs, attitudes, traditions and perspectives? Your values play a critical part in forming the foundation of self-image and identity. Values establish the standards that govern your life. There are many values that could shape your life, and some are more essential than others. High standards and excellence is a treasure for leaders who wish to unlock their leadership greatness. If you live your life or conduct yourself based on your values, they will help create your image and reputation. Your values may include:

- Achievement, artistic expression, belonging, character, competency, competitiveness, creativity, credibility, excellence, fairness, family, financial security, freedom, friendship, generosity, humor, health, identity, importance, inclusion, independence, integrity, learning, leadership

- Love, loyalty, organization, order, peace, perseverance, personal development, pleasure, power, recognition, relationship, religion, reputation, respect, self respect, tradition, wealth

What will you stand for? What will you support? What are the principles you live by and hold close to your heart? Your actions should be in line with your values, personal image and family reputation. When I asked a group of students to give an example of one of their most guiding principles, I got a broad range of answers. One person said it was important to him never to bring shame on his family name. Colin Powell, in his autobiography, spoke of this when he discussed growing up as a kid. There were certain things that were out of the question. He did not want to embarrass or bring shame on his family for there were consequences. In his autobiography, My American Journey, General Colin Powell said, "I never smoked marijuana, never got high, in fact never experimented with any drugs. And for a simple reason; my folks would have killed me."[1]

Parents may admonish their children and claim, "You are not going to embarrass me." They are concerned about the family's image. General Powell provided additional insight when he said, "If the values seem correct or relevant, the children will follow the values." Children understand and appreciate the need to avoid embarrassment. They do not want their parents to embarrass them in front of their friends. I spoke to my son's class when he was in fourth grade. I could tell that he was more nervous than I was about my performance. He did not want me to embarrass him in front of his friends. He wanted to belong and to be accepted and was concerned about his image and reputation.

Sometimes what is important to you is your own point of view. You may be self-centered, which is natural. There are times, however, when you realize that you should step out of your shoes and step into the shoes of another person. When you look at the world through the eyes of others, you gain a different sense on what is important. Imagine thinking like your parents on a certain issue and trying to figure out why they feel the way they do. It could be eye opening. There is a quote from Mark Twain that is very appropriate. Twain said, "When I was a boy of 14, my father was so ignorant I could hardly stand to have the old man around. But when I got to be 21, I was astonished at how much the old man had learned in seven years."[2]

Often you hear that life is not fair. I ask people why they feel life is not fair. They will say things like:

- Bad things happen to good people
- You work hard and someone else gets the credit
- Things don't go as planned
- The bad guys seem to get ahead and the good guys finish last
- We are not paid what we are worth

- Some people get away with murder
- Love is not returned
- People can't afford the medical care they need

There are many responses to this question, but it is good to step back and ask a question. Are you fair? People have invested a lot into your life. Are they getting a fair return? Your parents, teachers and coaches want you to succeed. Your parents likely made innumerable sacrifices on your behalf. Some parents immigrated to this country for a better life. Others marched and fought against injustices so that you could benefit. But have you been fair? Have you done your fair share? Have you treated people fairly? Have you treated your dreams, and those who had expectations and dreams for you, with the proper respect?

Is excellence important to you? The athlete or artist is consumed with many perfect moves and perfect strokes. Are you satisfied with your grades or work performance? Do they represent your best effort? What will you do about it? Why are you holding back your best effort? What are you waiting for to release your full talents? Be Excellent Start Today: BEST. Consider your major. Do you have a major that will lead to a specific job? Some students choose majors as they choose hobbies and never consider its income potential. When you choose a major, think of how it will meet your financial needs.

Is your belief in God important to you? Things that are important to you should be reflected in your lifestyle, words and actions. People asked to rate the top three areas of their life have often respond God first, family second and work/school third. Maybe you have a similar rating order. When you look at where you spend your time, thoughts and attention, is that priority ranking reflected? Take a few moments to reflect on the following poem called "Priorities." Consider how you might adjust the way you prioritize the important activities in your life.

Priorities

Take some time and fill in the blanks,
3 Reasons for which you give thanks,
Then study how your time is spent
And if it matches your intent.

Then list the values that define
Your life and rank them 1 to 9.
List the answers that you prefer,
Then ask a friend if they concur.

Initially you would reject,
The things we cherish we neglect.
When we inquire and inspect
We find there is a disconnect
Between intentions and the real;
The way we act on what we feel.

Take some time to explore your life.
You may want to get more of life.
And make sure that your time is spent,
So that it matches your intent.

Copyright © 2000 Orlando Ceaser

Relationships

Relationships are the center of our existence. Do your friends share your high standards? Jim Rohn, a motivational speaker said, "You are the average of the five people you spend the most time with."[3] Choose your friends wisely; your friends are often a reflection of your character.

People who love you have influence over you to a certain degree. They appreciate and have high expectations for your life. Sometimes they exert too much control and influence and want to direct every action. This is generally because they want the best for you. They want you to be successful. Be gentle with them. In time, you can bring them around to the goals you have set for your life.

Abraham Maslow, a famous psychiatrist says what is important to you is linked to your needs. You may have read about him in your psychology and business classes. He developed a pyramid, which shows the five major need groups. He said you must work from the bottom of the pyramid and complete or fulfill each level before moving to the next group, until you reach the top.[4] The five groups are:

- Physiological needs — food, clothing, and shelter
- Safety needs — protection
- Belonging needs
- Self-esteem needs
- Self Actualization needs

Maslow's Hierarchy of Needs

Self Actualization

Aesthetic and cognitive needs
knowledge, understanding, goodness, justice beauty,order, symmetry

Esteem needs
competence, approval, recognition

Belongingness and love needs
affiliation, acceptance, affection

Safety needs
security, physiological safety

Physiological needs
food, drink

What is important are the people and things that meet unmet needs. This may explain why you make some of your good and bad decisions. If something is important to you, you must be serious about it. If it is missing, you need to make sure it is covered. As you move through the steps on Maslow's chart, you may have to change and make adjustments to protect your position and meet your needs.

Bad Decisions — Pay Now or Pay Later

Bad decisions will haunt you for many years. Therefore, it is critical to think carefully before you act. Do not let people trap you into doing something wrong. The information channels are filled with stories of famous people who seemed to have it all: fame, money and a good reputation. These reasonably intelligent people violated trust and lost some things very valuable to them. You know the value of a good reputation and the difference between right and wrong.

I developed the chart below to show a graph of a person's career and the impact of poor decisions. There is a beginning phase, a growth phase and a point where an individual is at the top of their game. There are many points along the curve where they can make a mistake and crash to the ground. Those who reach the top of their profession have a long drop to the bottom. They have expertise, prestige and a tremendous reputation to uphold. Ego and poor judgment can lead to arrogance and destruction. As sad as their fall is to watch, it is more tragic when a young adult falls at the beginning of their career. You may not have far to fall to the bottom, but you may never reach the top of your dream career if you make a bad decision.

Career Growth & Poor Decisions

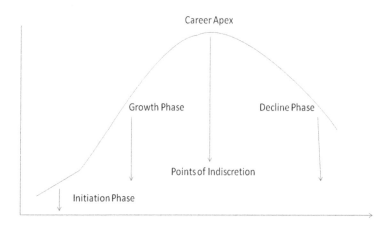

Copyright © 2010 Watchwell Communications, Inc.   www.watchwellinc.com

When you are tempted to violate your values or the law, remember the consequences stated on the graph of Career Growth and Poor Decisions. Many careers have been stunted before they started. You have so much to give to the world, so be wise and concentrate on your contributions and their potential benefits. Additionally, you have the capacity to influence a large number of people. If your reputation is destroyed and your career is stunted, it could adversely affect thousands of people.

Sailing or Settling

I am preparing notes for a high school commencement address. Two of the contrasting images I am considering are sailing through life and settling for whatever life presents to us. Sailing reminds me of being on the water, adjusting the sails to capitalize on the strength of the wind and the current. Settling brings to mind a house that is built on ground that is shifting. Settling also means to compromise and pretend to be satisfied with outcomes that are less than your original expectations.

Sailing requires someone to be in charge of the boat. The operator of the boat is responsible for the craft. You keep it properly maintained and fit for travel. You have expertise gained from many hours of practice. Your comfort level and sailing ability will turn most of your actions into routine decisions. You are in control; responding to the environment. Mastery of your surroundings is used to make better decisions. You are the captain or co-pilot steering in the direction of your destination. The last lines of the poem Invictus by William Ernest Henley, describe your emotions: "I am the master of my fate; I am the captain of my soul."[5]

When you are sailing in life, there is a confidence that comes from studying the wind and the waves, while learning from its instructions and instructors. When you are sailing through life, you should constantly gauge your position. You may approach the end of the day, reflect on progress and review your charts for tomorrow. You update your daily log and plan your strategies. Dr. Wayne Dyer speaks of reviewing the last 10 minutes of each day. He suggests that 10 minutes before you go to sleep is a good time to program or suggest to your subconscious mind a menu of options to review during sleep.[6] The concept revolves around the notion that you will get more of what you think about, whether they are positive or negative. You can influence the quality of your life through influencing your thinking.

In the book Checklist Manifesto, author Atul Gawande posits the belief that you can improve any result by developing a well-designed checklist. He told of a study in a hospital where infection rates were reduced drastically by the doctors' actions of reviewing a checklist before each surgery. Everyone in the upper room knew the correct procedure for preparing for surgery. Nevertheless, when a checklist was developed and nurses held accountable for ensuring that everyone followed the procedures, the impact was phenomenal. In one hospital, 43 infections and 8 deaths were prevented and $2 million were saved.[7] A checklist may enable you to sail through life, staying on task, reminding you of your promises, noting your position and making the necessary adjustments to reach a destination.

Settling, on the other hand, shows that you abandoned your original objective. You are convinced that your current state will have to be sufficient, because it is the best you will produce. It is not, "I am going to quit while I am ahead," but "I am going to quit instead, before I get hurt, or waste more time." You may be afraid of losing the small amount of gain that you have accomplished.

When you settle, you do not live up to your original dreams. Picture a house shifting and sinking into place due to a foundation that is not finished moving. It may eventually set itself into a permanent position. Remember the dog in Aesop's fable that lacks persistence. He tried to obtain fruit from a tree, but stops prematurely, saying the fruit was probably sour anyway. People who settle convince themselves that the prize was no longer worth pursuing. Why do people settle for less than they deserve? You can never say for sure, because the reasons vary with each individual and with each situation. Below are some common reasons:

Why People Settle

- Impatience – They were not willing to pay the price in time or resources

- Misjudged investment – The cost in time and resources is more or longer than expected

- Lack of Knowledge – They did not know the information needed to accomplish the objective

- Insufficient Resources – They did not have what was required to achieve the goal

- Lack of Confidence – They don't believe they deserve more and so they are satisfied with whatever they receive

You can usually spot when someone has settled for less by their actions and the content of their conversations. They may exhibit the following symptoms:

Symptoms of Settling
- Defensive — Very sensitive and do not want to be questioned
- Rationalizing — Deliver elaborate reasons to justify their actions
- Arrogance — May appear superior in their decision making, to hide insecurities about their decision
- Overzealous — Overly enthusiastic as they try to sell others on why it was the right idea, action or decision

You also must realize that settling may be a wise use of time. You may have other priorities that move higher on your list of objectives. It may be smart to cut your losses because the time investment may not be worth it.

The quality of your life depends, in part, on the choices you make. You may elect to adopt a sailing mentality, where you are in ship shape, prepared to handle the journey you imagined. Conversely, you may choose to settle and essentially surrender to the forces you face without a fight. When viewing and reviewing your life, take your inspiration from the sailing metaphor. May you face the challenges and opportunities and master the elements in a manner consistent with your purpose and your preparation, as you unlock your leadership greatness.

Reputation — Working Capital In A Successful Life

You may have heard the phrase, "You are nothing like I expected," or "You are nothing like I was told." When you heard those statements, you probably received them with mixed emotions. They could indicate positive feelings about you or an underlying misconception or suspicion about your reputation. Why were they surprised?

If you are like me, you try very hard to establish and protect your reputation. Your reputation is who you are, what you stand for and what you represent. Many times it goes before you and people say such things as, "Your reputation preceded you." Therefore, it is critical that you do everything to maintain a positive reputation.

Your reputation is like money. It helps you get benefits and special treatment, assignments, employment and academic opportunities. An excellent reputation affords you the benefit of the doubt and opens the door to information, power and influence. Reputation can affect what people think of you, for better or for worse. It can indicate that you are a fine person or someone others would not want to work with if you were the last person on Earth. Failing to pay attention to your reputation can be a very costly enterprise. A poor reputation may literally cost you influential internship opportunities. You may lose thousands of dollars in lost promotions, salary increases, bonuses, key relationships and important clients.

A Bad Reputation

Often, a bad or compromised reputation can have a surprising or difficult to pinpoint source. For example, a bad driving record, poor credit history or provocative statements on social media may result in unknown damage to your reputation. Many employers use background and credit checks and social media account reviews to access your suitability for their positions. Missteps in these areas can haunt your work life. You may miss a job opportunity because of something a potential employer discovered about you online. Unfortunately, that potential employer will likely never tell you the true reason why you were not offered a particular position.

There are other times when your poor reputation may be due to someone else's ill behavior. A candidate that I know was almost denied employment because his previous supervisor misrepresented his reputation during a reference check. The new company was so impressed with him in the interview that they allowed him an opportunity to address the malicious accusations lodged against him. He told his version of the story to address the example his employer had given, which was completely taken out of context. He also supplied the names of others within his organization, the zone manager and director of sales. They both spoke very highly of the candidate and even went as far as to discredit his supervisor, thus enabling him to get the job. This does not usually happen, but the reputation of the candidate came through loudly and clearly in the interview. He was honest and forthright in his assessment of his performance. He was very convincing and had references to support his reputation and version of his performance.

While you are working hard to protect your reputation, bear in mind there may be individuals trying to give you a bad name. There are detractors or haters, determined to bring you down and remove you from competing with them for a current or future assignment. A director was instructed to hire an assistant. The person under consideration was someone who had competed against her for her current job. She was initially reluctant to make the appointment. She had the usual concerns about this individual potentially sabotaging her agenda. However, she was open to using the person's skills to improve her department's overall performance. She also felt that she could groom the individual to one day take her job or a similar assignment. She accepted it as a good challenge.

Shortly after the person joined her department, she began hearing from members of the team about the negative comments her new assistant was making about her. He secretly questioned her decisions and even went as far as to sabotage some of their projects. Additionally, he was personally connected to other directors and began to influence their perceptions of her. He told them she was lazy, incompetent and ineffective and that she was in a job that was over her head. They believed him because he worked closely with her. He wanted her out of the job so he could take her place. He could not beat her in the interview, but he was committed to poisoning her reputation. She eventually reassigned him, but it was too late to prevent the damage to her reputation.

Tips for Maintaining an Excellent Reputation

A positive reputation is crucial in validating who you are. It is a reflection of your life's work and therefore you must guard it as you would your bank account or investment portfolio. It is essential that your actions are above and beyond reproach so as to support your reputation. In this manner, you will establish a history of consistency that can offer up as evidence in the event someone tries to sabotage your character. You must not cut corners where integrity is concerned. You do not want anyone to doubt your character.

The people you claim as friends and associates influence your reputation. Be careful and mindful of your friends. The way in which they are perceived, whether positively or not, may influence how others perceive you. Similarly, your affiliations may reflect upon your character. Be sure to align yourself with organizations that have positive reputations and are known for excellence and great service.

You must do everything in your power to keep your reputation positive and of the highest caliber. This involves monitoring and managing your personal and professional image. Just as there are agencies to monitor your credit and issue credit reports, you must find a way to monitor your reputation. You must set up a process, a mechanism or system to collect image data on yourself. Below are a few simple techniques you should consider.

— Reputation Feedback

Select a few trusted friends, colleagues and academic advisors to give you feedback on your character, image and personal leadership. These factors all add up to your reputation as a whole. You may use any method you choose to gather information, either by questionnaire, on the telephone, in a meeting or over a meal. In addition, in the case of face-to-face meetings, remember to look for non-verbal feedback as well. Consider asking the following questions:

- Do you believe I am a thoughtful listener?
- Do you feel I that treat you and others fairly?
- Have you heard anything about me that should be brought to my attention?
- What are things I need to change to make things better for you?
- Am I reliable? Trustworthy? Credible?
- Is there any dissent that has surfaced about my leadership style?
- What can I do to make you feel a greater part of the team?
- Are my actions in line with my stated values and intentions and your expectations?

Ask different people about the word on the street about you. What are people saying? What have they heard about you?

You should always be aware of your actions because they are registered somewhere in the hearts and minds of those around you. The collection of your actions will shape your reputation and place you in high esteem or doom you to suffer dire consequences.

- The old adage of "your word is your bond" should have meaning in your life, as you follow through on your obligations
- Treat people the way you want to be treated

- Remember you are always on duty, as a representative of your family, school and companies

- Always model and uphold your personal and family values

- Do not do anything that you would not like to see as a headline in the media

- Cultivate a number of trusted individuals who will advise you on matters that may affect your career

- Cultivate advocates who will defend your reputation and alert you to any assaults on your character

You can bolster your character, image and reputation by sticking to these cardinal principles to keep your positive reputation as a valuable asset.

Tiebreakers — Beating the Crowd In A Photo Finish

In this world where sameness is celebrated, similarity is everywhere. Parity is another word used to describe sameness that exists among sports teams. A commodity is a product that customers believe will have the same quality and usefulness no matter which company sells the product. The competing companies' products are interchangeable and easily can be substituted one for the other. As with products on the market, the value of potential employees may be perceived as undifferentiated. If candidates are seen as equal, something must be done to break the tie, to establish an edge. A slight variation can be seen as an advantage.

There is an abundance of talented candidates applying for jobs and many have equivalent academic and professional skill sets and expertise. College admissions officers receive applications from a large number of straight "A" students and others with high grade point averages. Employment offices receive resumes from people with indistinguishable backgrounds. You have to devise a strategy to stand out, to differentiate yourself from the crowd. The strategy could be to increase your educational edge by obtaining an advanced degree or certificate of specialization in an area of need. You can also gain additional skills and experience through volunteer activities on the job, in school or in your community.

Leaders are needed in great numbers. Great leadership is desperately needed. Individuals with the emotional and intellectual fortitude to inspire and lead others to complete projects, exceed sales goals and solve problems will find employment. People with strong technical and social skills and emotional intelligence will always be in demand. Since many applicants have similar skills, experience and education, how will you break the tie in the employer's mind? How would you demonstrate that you are the leader they are seeking? What would you use as a tiebreaker if you were making a decision between several comparable people? This thought process will help you imagine what factors the interviewer is weighing.

Examples of potential tiebreakers may include the following:
- Unique or various experiences that set you apart from others
- Interests, hobbies and attributes that could add to the skills of your team. What are your interests that grow you in other areas? Your participation in volunteer activities

may indicate your tireless dedication to helping others. Creative hobbies, involving activities such as art and music, can portray an interesting person who can bring a unique perspective to problem solving.

- Sports can be a tiebreaker, particularly if you reached a high level of competency and can demonstrate valuable skills acquired during your playing days. The skills you may have acquired as the captain of your varsity volleyball team may be parlayed into leadership position at a potential employer.

- Some hiring personnel look for points of identification with the interviewee as a potential tiebreaker. I worked for a manager who loved to play racquetball. In one of our joint interviews, when all else was equal between the current and previous interviewee, I could sense that he was leaning toward the candidate who was an avid racquetball player.

- Someone who has worked through additional challenges. For example, one who works full time while carrying a full course load could be seen as someone with an exceptionally strong desire to succeed. Dave was a manager who worked his way through college and paid for 100% of his education. Not surprisingly, he gave extra points to candidates who had a similar experience. If he discovered this information during an interview, he immediately connected with the candidate. This played into the decision-making process. He would use this information to break a tie.

- Excellent communication skills can set you apart from the
  group. You will enhance your profile by taking advantage
  of opportunities to communicate in a variety of scenarios.
  Do not shy away from situations where you are tasked
  with presenting your ideas to others in formal and informal
  settings. A future employer will often look at these activities
  as an example of your having the extra skill set to lead
  teams and positively influence others.

The above are just a few factors that may help break the tie between
you and another equally impressive candidate. In these early stages
of your career development, think about acquiring extracurricular
activities and education that could prove instrumental in your
career trajectory. The more well rounded you are, the greater the
possibility of breaking the tie with other candidates.

I attended a conference years ago and heard Tony Alessandra,
PhD. discuss the need for leaders to work on their depth and
breadth of knowledge.[8] The depth of knowledge is the body of
information in your chosen area of interest: the data, experiences
and connections that are the basis of your expertise in your area
of specialization. Your breadth of knowledge is all of the other
things you know outside of your business that makes you a more
well rounded and more interesting person.

Your career plan should contain elements or characteristics to set
you apart from others. As you examine your interests and skills,
ask yourself, "Who would be interested in this array of talent? Am
I competitive enough? What is missing? What do I need to do
short term and long term?" If interviewing were compared to a

horse race, there would be people scattered all over the track. However, many would cross the line in a photo finish. It is up to the interviewers to find meaningful ways to separate the candidates with equivalent skills. They find a way to break the tie. Illustrating and demonstrating your diverse skills, talents, background and connections will help them break the tie in your favor.

Discussions Topics for Personal Reflection and Small Groups

1. List the top 5 to 10 areas of your life and rank them in order of importance.

2. What role do these areas have in your daily living, including the amount of time spent on each?

3. Recall the last time your values were tested and how you reacted to the challenge.

4. Recall a time when you disappointed someone who was on your side. How did you make it up to them? How did you apologize for your actions? Has the relationship returned to normal?

5. Discuss the Career Growth & Poor Decisions Chart. Where are you on the chart? Where do you want to be? Discuss a person in the news who recently fell because of character issues.

6. Discuss the ways you have seen someone destroy or damage their reputation. What can someone do to repair a damaged image?

7. What can you do to distinguish yourself from others who seem comparable to you in their school performance?

CHAPTER 6

ALWAYS BE CREATIVE (ABC)

Encourage new ideas by inspiring new ways to study, work and play

"Your imagination is your preview of life's coming attractions."

—Albert Einstein

"Is it that school taught us some things that we will never use or we will never use some of the things that school has taught us?"

—Orlando Ceaser

"Don't think. Thinking is the enemy of creativity. It's self-conscious, and anything self-conscious is lousy. You can't try to do things. You simply must do things."

—Ray Bradbury

Creativity is the ability to see something that others may not see. It is not restricted to musicians, artists, singers, writers, actors and architects. Students initiated modern advancement in social media and computer innovations. Individuals such as Michael Dell, Bill Gates and Mark Zuckerberg were students when they activated their dreams that revolutionized the world. Walt Disney, from an earlier generation, was also motivated as a student to change the status quo.

Creative is defined as:

1. Having the ability to create

2. Characterized by originality of thought; having or showing imagination: *a creative mind*

3. Designed to or tending to stimulate the imagination: *creative toys*

4. Characterized by sophisticated bending of the rules or conventions: *creative accounting* (source: Collins English Dictionary Online)

Creativity is an attribute that you may not believe you possess. However, if you objectively review your life, you will recognize situations and events where you used creativity to solve problems. You should internalize that creative problem-solving ability as a directive, a command to think of a better solution, a mandate to find a better way.

Creativity is personal and everyone has a different way of expressing it. Never compare your level of creativity to someone else's or you will run the risk of stifling your own growth. I once doubted my creativity. I almost stopped writing one year when I compared my writing ability to one of my fellow students. My classmate used the phrase "her hair was like the floating sands of the desert." I thought that phrase was so beautiful. I could never write anything rivaling its simplicity and poetic splendor. However, I continued to write, but labored under the belief that I would always be second rate. One day while reading a book of famous poets, I came across that same phrase in a book written by one of the giants of poetry. My classmate had "borrowed" the phrase from someone else. I almost torpedoed my writing career by comparing my gift to that of another poet. Creativity, like beauty, is in the eyes of the beholder.

Creativity is Critical

Creativity is an important part of your everyday life. In a world where knowledge is exploding every day and the number of people competing for the same opportunities is growing, there is a need to discover a competitive advantage. Creativity is one skill where leaders differentiate themselves from the rest of the challengers. Often people are afraid to take risks and this leads to duplications of the things that are popular and successful. Your creativity as a leader separates you from your peers. Your creativity will lead to the development of programs, new initiatives and innovations that will enable you to stand apart from those around you.

De Witt Jones, former photographer with National Geographic magazine, refers to creativity as an attitude. He says, "Creativity is looking at the ordinary and seeing the extraordinary."[1] Cultivating this talent will enable you to make significant contributions to classroom discussions, potential business opportunities and job performance. In order to unlock your leadership greatness, it is essential to exploit all of your talents.

Creativity is often misunderstood and underutilized. Many believe it to be only for those in the arts. When you adopt a creative mindset, however, you will open the door to amazing possibilities. My creative process has two simple drivers: I am always open to the activities in my environment and I use my downtime for creative exploration. I am very aware of what goes on around me. My surroundings are full of motion that traps and ensnares my thoughts. Mentally, I am constantly called out to play and invited to fish for new ideas. I believe that you can learn from everything and everybody and that everything and everybody can teach you something. I take full advantage of these learning opportunities. I keep a notepad on the nightstand next to my bed. If I am awakened at night, I want to be sure that I can record any dreams or ideas that may be useful in a later context. While sitting in meetings, I discover some of my best ideas. When there is a lull in the meeting or the topic does not require my full attention, I may use the time to observe other participants or to think of something interesting. While driving or sitting on a train, I use these excellent opportunities to think of ideas or to solve problems. My downtime is my mental playtime and I use it to the best of my ability.

Creativity is a trigger that challenges your current reality and asks you to look at the world or problems differently. Ask yourself the following questions routinely:

- Is this the best way to perform this task or solve this problem?

- Is there another way to do it? What is a new and different way to achieve the same or better results that is more efficient and costs less money?

- How can I improve this product or service?

- How can I look at this problem through fresh eyes?

- Can I apply information or a technique from another industry or from another department to make this work better?

Creativity leads to the generation of lots of ideas. Linus Pauling, the Nobel Prize winning chemist said, "The way to get good ideas is to get lots of ideas, and throw the bad ones away."[2] Pharmaceutical companies, for example, will usually screen and test close to 10,000 compounds before they settle on two drugs to develop to market. If you are always observing and always thinking, you will increase your chances of having a large volume of ideas from which to choose.

Benefits, Barriers and Breakthroughs

There are benefits, barriers and breakthroughs when you generate, evaluate and implement creative ideas. Be creative to initiate and sustain a competitive advantage. Be creative to unlock your leadership greatness.

Benefits

- Helps you solve problems with new solutions
- Enables you to adjust to a changing world and changing circumstances
- Helps you to view the world through a wide angled lens in search of new ideas
- Allows you to see things differently, with new patterns and associations
- Allows you to connect with yourself and others
- Helps build relationships, as you share your ideas with others
- Promotes personal discovery
- Connects you with the joy and fulfillment from using your innate desire to build and create
- Relaxes and reduces stress

Roger von Oech, an internationally recognized leader in stimulating creativity and innovation, developed the barriers described below:

Barriers to Creativity
- You lock onto what you call 'The right answer'
- You say, "That's not logical" — you are overly critical in brainstorming session to new ideas
- Follow the rules to a fault
- Suggest people be practical as a means to stifle risk taking
- Label play as frivolous — scorn the outrageous which can eliminate options
- That's not my area — refuse to look to other areas for ideas
- Don't be foolish — in response to suggestions or as a guideline
- Avoid ambiguity
- Discourage making mistakes
- I'm not creative — believing this false statement[3]

Breakthroughs
- You are astonished by your ability to create
- You realize that you have shown this gift of problem solving throughout your life
- You recognize that suspending judgment keeps you open to new possibilities
- Your creative self talk places an expectation in your mind to generate new ideas

- You wake up with new solutions to your problems by reviewing them ten minutes before going to bed

Creative Execution

We have many goals that are steps to one desired result. A series of goals may look like a row of low hurdles on a straightaway or around a curve on a racing track. Pacing is required between hurdles. You must maintain the proper speed and exert the appropriate effort for successful clearance. Hurdles have adjustable bars and may be low or high depending on the race. While hurdles are evenly spaced in athletic competition, hurdles in life, school or business may not be as predictable. They may be close together at times and far apart at other times. Some hurdles may seem to spring into your path without warning. One point is very clear: you need proper training and conditioning to develop skills to perform well in life, which can sometimes feel like a veritable steeplechase.

The game often changes, as the competition gets wiser, tougher and more aggressive. The demands of instructors, employers and customers are greater. The bar is higher. You find yourself "high jumping" goals that once only required hurdle-jumping skills. The annual event seems to occur more frequently. You have to train and condition vigorously to be successful. You must stress mental and physical muscles and develop stamina for longer races as well as the speed and energy bursts for sprints. Yesterday's training routine is not enough.

Creativity may be necessary to clear the bar. You may have to include variety, flexibility and versatility in your training regimen or change your techniques. High jumping, as a competitive sport, became popular in England in the 1800s. High jumping has gone through several evolutions in techniques over the years. Since its introduction into the United States, each new development in high jumping techniques ruled for a number of years before the next iteration became commonplace. The main techniques were the Scissors (1874), the Eastern Cut-off (1892), the Western roll (1912), The Straddle (1930), the Dive Straddle (1960) and the Fosbury Flop (1967).

Dick Fosbury was a high jumper at Oregon State University in the 1960s. He was not terribly successful as a high jumper until he changed his technique. The Fosbury Flop revolutionized high jumping and enabled Dick Fosbury to break the world's record at the Mexico City Olympics games in 1968, with a 7 foot 4.25-inch jump. His success led to others duplicating his form and replicating his results. Whereas, there were several styles in action before he won, the day after his victory, everyone was trying the Fosbury Flop and it continues to be the dominant style.[4]

Just as other high jumpers adopted the Fosbury Flop, businesses tend to build on well-established methods. Companies will use similar systems through their habit of best practices sharing, identical training and using the same consultants. If a methodology is effective, its use will be widely adopted. Innovation is a continuous process. Triumphs may be short lived. Dedication to creating new processes and ways of working and serving better is critical.

The bar is indeed higher. Our discussion has gone from hurdle jumping to high jumping. Eventually, your goals may demand the skills of a pole-vaulter. The goal is well over your head and you need resources, a pole, to help you clear the bar. In early pole vaulting, athletes used poles made of ash (wood). As the demands for higher heights grew, the sport adopted poles made from bamboo, aluminum and finally different versions of fiberglass. Your pole, in school or at work, may be a new idea, process, more or different resources, new strategies, routines, tactics, attitudes, products or services. Vaulting skills must be added on to the hurdling and high jumping skills learned earlier through experience. The right tool in your hand will give you the confidence to run down the straightaway and to clear the bar.

Discussion Topics for Personal Reflection and Small Groups

1. What is the greatest risk you have ever taken and what did you learn from it?

2. What are your habits and interests?

3. What is your best idea or suggestion to make something better?

4. Do you consider yourself a creative person, and if not, why not?

5. Have you ever thought of a way to do something differently? What was it and how did it make you feel?

CHAPTER 7

EXECUTE WITH PASSION

*Aggressively implements plans and
checklists to stay on tasks*

"I've missed more than 9,000 shots in my career.
I've lost almost 300 games. 26 times, I've been
trusted to take the game winning shot and missed.
I've failed over and over and over again in my life.
And that is why I succeed."

—Michael Jordan

"Success is often fear in motion."

—Orlando Ceaser

"Emphasize your strengths on your resume, in your
cover letters and in your interviews. It may sound
obvious, but you'd be surprised how many people
simply list everything they've ever done. Convey your
passion and link your strengths to measurable results.
Employers and interviewers love concrete data."

—Marcus Buckingham

Cocky & Rhodette

I don't mind bending over backwards for my customers, it's the bending over forward that makes me nervous.

As illustrated in the above graphic, sometimes you will need to go the extra mile to prove your commitment to a task. To execute with passion, you will need to be steadfast in your commitment. When times are tough, the weak get nervous and lose focus, often imagining the worst-case scenario. In their minds, the sky is always falling. The strong, however, will show that in every bad situation there is the seed of an equal or greater benefit. They look for the gifts and opportunities to shine, to make a difference and to provide greater service to others.

You must be persistent in your ability to carry out assignments. In their book Execution, Larry Bossidy and Ram Charan described execution as a discipline. "Execution is a specific set of behaviors and techniques that companies need to master in order to have a competitive advantage."[1] Create a culture, a way of thinking and acting that achieves stellar results. This book emphasizes the value of having a strong knowledge of self. This self-awareness allows you to monitor your impact on people. Self-mastery gives you the control necessary to make adjustments. Be authentic so that people know that what they see is what they will get. You should ensure that there is no need for others to guess about where you stand on an issue and how you will perform. Use humility as a leadership trait, which enables people to follow you with a complete understanding of your passion for executing to get outstanding results.

Jack Welch and Suzy Welch, in their book Winning, discuss the power of execution to complete the overall performance picture. They say, "Being able to execute is a special and distinct skill. It means a person knows how to put decisions into action and push them forward to completion, through resistance, chaos, or unexpected obstacles. People who can execute know that winning is about results."[2]

You must understand the landscape on which you operate. Evaluate and anticipate the competition's past, present and potential future responses. Run scenarios on potential barriers to execution and devise a means to neutralize any possible obstacles. If you are working in a team, drive home the importance of paying attention to details with your fellow team members. This emphasis will allow them to follow through on a well-developed goal and plan. The result will be extraordinary. Continue to be passionate in your drive to exceed the objectives outlined in your blueprint. You will develop a reputation for getting things done and done in a spectacular manner, which attracts the attention of future employers, peers and those in higher leadership positions within your organization.

Success Attitudes

You have heard that attitude is everything. Your mental framework for your goals has a direct impact on your performance. The key to proper framing is to adopt a point of view that allows you to play a role in the solution. When faced with a challenging situation, do not say, "it can't be done." Instead, you should say, "it hasn't been done yet." From this point, you should begin to think of ways to make it happen. If you think that others just do not understand, reframe your thoughts to "those folks don't get it, yet." This allows for hope and trust for change in the future. Now you are in a position to work toward a solution of helping those people understand your vision. Complaining without solutions or actions is not productive and is not consistent with an attitude for success.

Many of the solutions to your problems are in the way you think about them. Your thinking will predict the way you act and how you will perform. Take a moment and review your thoughts about the future. Remember to frame the challenge so that you have a role in the solution. If you feel you are powerless and nothing can be done, then you will have no power and nothing will be done.

Independent Thinking

Cocky & Rhodette — by Orlando Ceaser

I woke up one day and was consumed by this burning desire to go to work and think for myself.

You should be in charge of your thoughts. This is especially important as your thoughts generally dictate your actions, for better or for worse. Consider the following quotations, each of which emphasize the power of thoughts and their impact on solutions:

> "Today is a reflection of yesterday's thinking. Tomorrow will reflect how you think today. Think lovingly, positively, and as though anything is possible... and it will be."

> **—Marianne Williamson**

"The significant problems we face cannot be solved at the same level of thinking as when we created them."

—Albert Einstein

"Failures are divided into two classes — those who thought and never did and those who did and never thought."

—John Charles Salak

As an independent thinker, you must be wary of those who want to control the way you think. These people may be peers who desire to have control over everyone around them. They may attempt to manipulate your thinking for their own personal gain or satisfaction. This is not to suggest that there is always a sinister motive. It could be merely that they like to have everyone agree with them. If you are not careful, you may follow their advice and believe it is your own. You do not want to be hostage to the desires, whims and suggestions of others. You must follow your own thoughts. Remember, your thoughts are what guide your actions and you want them to guide you toward your ultimate goals. You must examine all of the evidence and information available to make a well-informed decision on the matters that will keep you moving forward in a positive and productive manner.

The Know System™ for Decision-Making

Systems are the keys to accomplishment and personal growth. You need a system to remind you of commitments and to structure your thinking to make better decisions. I developed The Know System to help users gather information to solve problems and focus on priorities. I introduced this system in Chapter 4 in connection with time management strategies. The principles are applicable to numerous decisions, projects and questions.

I was walking through a terminal at O'Hare airport in Chicago on a business trip. I saw an advertisement that contained the word KNOW in bold letters. The word "KNOW" stood out against the white fluorescent background and the word stuck in my mind. As I walked further down the concourse I saw another sign on the right hand side of the corridor with the same simple message, KNOW. The word seemed to talk to me and reached out to me. I still had a long walk before I arrived at my gate, so I began playing games with the word. I turned the word inside out and rearranged the letters. I wondered how many words were in this word and was surprised at how many there were. The most common words found in the word KNOW are:

- Know, Now, No, On, Own, OK, Wok, Won, KO and Ow

The Know System has four broad categories: Data, Goal, Focus and Action.

The Know System™

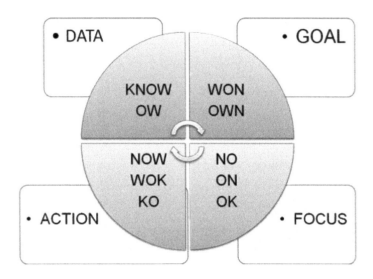

Data

— Know

When making decisions, there is information you know and information you need to know. By asking the right questions of the right people, you explore one of your greatest resources. You were taught as a child to use who, what, when, where, why and how to ask questions. These key words fit perfectly into the KNOW component.

- Who do you know that can help you?

- What do you know and what do you need to know?

- When do you need the information?
- Where do you need to go to find what you need to know?
- How will you obtain the information you need to know?
- Why do you need to know?
- What do you know about your dream?
- What do you know about yourself?
- Do you know what your success will look like?
- Who do you know that has your desired job?
- Do you know what it will take to reach your dream?
- Do you know the cost of success?

These questions are excellent guidelines for the research necessary to obtain data to reach your dreams. They will prod you to examine your knowledge base and pinpoint your knowledge deficiencies. This will set you up to ask the right questions and improve your thinking.

– Ow

Ow is the cry you utter when something hurts you. Pain is a symptom, the body's way or a system's way of showing you that something is wrong. You may feel physical pain if you are using the wrong technique to exercise. You may feel the pain of lower grades if your study habits are lacking. Further, you may feel the pain of missed promotions if you are not putting in the requisite effort on your job. Then again, pain can also be the natural discomfort you go through when you grow, change or try something new. You must be able to tell the difference between the two and react accordingly. In other words, sometimes the pain tells you to make adjustments for better outcomes and, at other times, you must soldier through the pain in order to get closer to your goals.

Goal

— Won

The objective of every competition is to win. When you say, "I won," you are stating success against a particular standard. Have you established what your success looks like and what it means to be victorious? Do you have a goal in sight? In order to win, aside from the effort you will need to put forth, you must have a clear goal and knowledge of where the finish line is located. In setting out your winning plan, know that there will be milestones along the way. Reaching these milestones, which are incremental accomplishments and victories toward the ultimate goal, must also be apart of your plan for winning.

— Own

You must be committed to get your best results. When you take responsibility or ownership for some project, you give it your full attention and energy. You own up to the challenge and declare your desire to complete the task. You are accountable. You will fight to make your dream a reality. Owning also shows the maturity of the person involved. You are aware of the value of the situation and will step up and perform your best. If you adopt an owner's way of thinking, you are more concerned for the people and the projects you are working on. You must make sure all of the resources are present and in working order. You also must follow through on all of your commitments so that others, whom you may need to rely upon, recognize that you are serious.

- You need to own your dream

- You must be committed to making it work, for yourself, your family and, if applicable, your team members

- Having confidence in yourself and owning your dreams and plans for your future are the keys to achieving your best

Focus

– *No*

You have to say no to some things and some people. You cannot be all things to all people and there will be times when you must stay focused on your goal. This will require you to develop the ability to resist anything that is not a priority. You may even have to say no to yourself if you find that you are spending too much time and energy on non-productive activities. Saying no to someone is often difficult, but you must develop this discipline to avoid the risk of not giving adequate attention to your school assignments, work projects and those other goals you have set as priorities.

- Who are the people you need to say no to?

- What are some things you need to say no to?

- Is there a mindset that you need to say no to? For example, do you need to say no to negative thinking that may lead you to believe that a certain task is too big or that you do not have the proper resources to complete it?

- Can you identify an instance in your past where saying no would have helped you get closer to your dream?

– On

You must be dedicated and focused on your assignment. You must be enthusiastic and energized. You, therefore, must be "on" at all times. When you are on target, on fire and turned on about something special, you attract the people and the resources you need. When you are on, your guard is always up and you protect that which is important to you. When you are around someone who is on, their passion is contagious and you want to be a part of their excitement. In order to be "on," you must be in constant contact with your power source. Whatever replenishes you and gives you energy should be close at hand and visited often.

- What really turns you on?

- What fuels your excitement?

- If you were on target, what would that look like?

- What is your source of energy: physical, mental, emotional and spiritual?

– Ok

Are your results OK, but they could be better? You need to ask yourself why that is. You deserve to be functioning at a higher degree. Jim Collins, in his book Good to Great, says that "good is the enemy of excellence."[3] If that is the case, OK must surely be another one of its enemies. The only time OK becomes satisfactory is when you are checking off your list. "Do I have all that I need? "Check." OK then becomes a nice way of keeping you mindful of your progress toward completing your mission.

Action

— Now

One of the early action steps you take toward your goal is information gathering. What are you going to do now? Now that you have this knowledge, what are you doing with it? Are your current actions in line with your goals? Are they helping to move you along toward achieving your dreams? It is critical to reflect at various steps on your journey to check your progress.

- What are you doing now to reach your dream?
- Have you put into action daily, weekly or monthly tasks that advance you toward your dream?
- Are your actions the most important things you can do right now?
- Are you unreasonably expecting an outcome now that may take more time and planning before it comes to fruition?

Additionally, you may ask yourself, "What am I doing now with my time?" "What is the situation now?" "How are things proceeding now?" The answers to these and similar questions are a way for you to evaluate your current situation and allow you to continue to adjust your actions and expectations for you future.

— Wok

The wok, a skillet used for preparing stir-fry and other dishes, is used here as a metaphor for variety. In a wok, a variety of food items are stirred, tossed and blended together. This method of cooking provides for complex layers of complementing flavors. Sometimes we have to stir things up a bit. Sometimes it is required to approach a subject from different angles. The fact that something was done one way for a long time does not mean it always has to be done that way. You need flexibility and variety to create new ways of operating. The status quo may be no longer adequate to meet the needs of a dynamic society. By being open to trying something novel, or even new combinations of existing models, you will be in a better position to take the status quo to newer and more exciting heights.

- Never be afraid to mix things up a bit
- You may have to stir things up until you find the right approach
- Creativity and innovation are born from experimentation
- Sometimes, you have to change your routine, expect change in your environment and learn how to adjust to change

– KO

In boxing, the term KO refers to a knockout. This occurs when a fighter falls to the floor and remains there, sometimes unconscious, for a count of eight seconds. There are other versions of the knockout: the standing eight count and the technical knockout (TKO), both of which are employed to protect the fighter who is deemed no longer able to physically or mentally defend themselves. If you are not prepared, mentally or physically, to compete in school or in the workplace, you risk a knockout from the game. You will be unprotected and open to the superior advantage of your competition. The term KO is also considered a winning combination. You want to be able to deliver the KO, whether it is acing your exams, nailing the interviews or the job assignments. You want to be on the side of the KO that is helpful and beneficial to you.

Discussion Topics for Personal Reflection or Small Groups

1. Think about a problem or project before you go to bed. Revisit the problem each morning. Do this for several nights, with the expectation of a solution. Record any breakthroughs in your approach to resolution.

2. Train your mind to work on your dreams throughout the day. Write down any ideas that come to you.

3. Select two decisions you have to make in the future. Develop a list of questions using the Know System.

4. What will you do differently? Will you write a journal or place a notepad by your bed to capture your thoughts?

CHAPTER 8

LEAD BY EXAMPLE

Personal actions should match your words

"Only those who will risk going too far can possibly find out how far one can go."

—T.S. Eliot

"Everyone who's ever taken a shower has an idea. It's the person who gets out of the shower, dries off and does something about it who makes a difference."

—Nolan Bushnell

"What you are speaks so loudly, I can't hear what you are saying."

—Ralph Waldo Emerson

You are being watched

"You are being watched. Observation can be an obstacle or an opportunity. Here are three questions to consider while contemplating a response. Can you use the attention and scrutiny to your advantage? Can you make a positive transformative statement about who you are? Can you alter perceptions and change minds and hearts by the power of your positive provocative performance?"

Someone is Watching

In earlier chapters, we discussed the need for you to develop your knowledge base, skills, self-awareness and time-management and networking abilities to help you attain your goals. Those skills are key to unlocking your leadership greatness. This chapter will discuss how your leadership qualities can be beneficial to those around you and lead to others' success. More often than not, we find ourselves working in teams or relying on others' knowledge, talents or efforts to accomplish a goal. As a leader, you want the best from others. You want to stand as a symbol of excellence to motivate and mobilize others to excel and always give their best effort.

In today's academic environment, the need for student leaders is particularly critical. Research has confirmed that about 50%

of U.S. college students take up to six years to obtain their four-year college degree. Similarly, for students embarking upon a 2-year associate's degree, only 29% of them received their degrees within three years of matriculation. Richard Arum and Josipa Roksa supply these statistics in their book Academically Adrift: Limited Learning on College Campuses. "Students are falling behind other countries in their academic skills. Professors are not challenging them enough and only 9% of their time is spent studying."[1]

There is a strong need for students who can lead by a positive example. A greater number of individuals must step forward and spend their time studying, making wise decisions around their study habits, personal behavior and taking courses that lead to a meaningful career. Andrew McAfee, in a report for the Harvard Business Review, writes, "Arum and Roksa found that in every college studied some students show great improvement on the CLA (Collegiate Learning Assessment which measures critical thinking). In general, these are students who spent more time studying (especially studying alone), took courses with more required reading and writing, and had more demanding faculty."[2] The need for you to unlock your leadership greatness, to inspire other students, is indeed great and can have far-reaching benefits.

Lead by example and know that someone is always watching you. Leadership qualities surface early in someone's academic and professional careers. People will notice as you begin to develop and unlock your leadership greatness, by the manner in which you inspire your peers. Further, unlocking your leadership greatness will attract similarly motivated people to your circle.

You must become the leader, to unlock your leadership greatness. You must stick to your values and your personal interpretation of self and you must stay out in front. People will try to persuade you to their way of thinking and acting, but it is your agenda and it is up to you to set the example. You must remain focused on your reason for being in college: to get a great education and prepare for your future contributions to yourself and to society.

Delaying Gratification

The will to delay gratification is a difficult one to exercise. Despite the decades old mantra "no pain, no gain," most people want to bypass the pain and go straight to the reward. People are fixated on the possibility of an early and high return from the smallest investment. They want the homerun at every turn at bat. They crave the diet plan that allows them to eat all they want and still lose weight. They want to believe that they can get rich quick, whether it is from playing the lottery or participating in the latest pyramid business venture. The perennial question is why do people have to have so much and so fast? Why does it have to be immediate?

I wonder if people are reluctant to delay gratification because they lack faith that their best effort will yield a commensurate return. Maybe they know people who have seemingly done all of the right things only to end up living a life of mediocrity. On the other hand, maybe they lack faith in themselves, not certain that they are capable of the persistence needed to reach their ultimate prize. As a result, they may gravitate toward that reward that requires the least output of time, energy and emotional investment. Great success seldom is attained by way of shortcuts.

You may not think about the fact that there is an adventure associated with delaying gratification. It is saving up for the big payoff, the holiday spurge, the ego boost, the ultimate satisfaction from a sense of achievement. You have to convince more people to sacrifice for the long term or you will have a cadre of unfulfilled people far south of their potential, settling for the timid return that matches their investment. As you lead by example, you will attract people to you, by your enthusiastic and hopeful manner in which you chase your dreams.

Instant Gratification

It is important to understand factors that may influence your behavior. The more you understand yourself the easier it is to predict how you will behave in the future. The graph below mimics the classic business growth curve for sales and profits. In the business context, the graph would represent a steady and consistent rise in sales and profits over a designated increment of time, such as months, quarters or years. I have developed a variation of the graph to demonstrate how satisfaction and related factors increase or decrease over time. The graph below depicts Satisfaction on the y-axis plotted against Time on the x-axis. Instant gratification is the desire to obtain satisfaction in the smallest amount of time. Everyone wants to get rich quick, to be an overnight sensation. On the graph, the steep line going almost straight up represent that desire. You may not have laid the proper foundation, put in the work, achieved the education or earned it, but you want the reward. Often, people who win the lottery or receive something of value that they did not expect or for which they did not plan fit into this category. Because this good fortune arrived before the individual had adequate time to plan how this reward would fit into their long-term plans, the person usually loses this treasure in a short period. Easy come, easy go. Since they did not have time and energy invested in the reward, they may not have fully appreciated the value of what they had. Ultimately, after the loss, they may level off at a low level of satisfaction. They will remain at this level for many years. They will have memories of their 15 minutes of fame, always reliving the good old days. If they do not adjust their expectations and tactics for achieving success, they will be doomed to a life of regrets and missed opportunities.

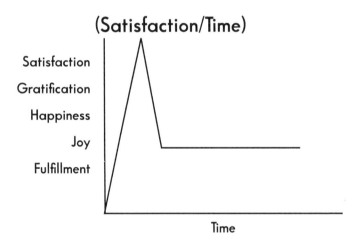

(Satisfaction/Time)

Satisfaction
Gratification
Happiness
Joy
Fulfillment

Time

Many people do not do the work, but deep in their hearts, they still want the prize. There may be students in class with you today who fit the bill. They will not do the work, follow the rules or pay their dues, yet they feel entitled to a good standard of living. This is unfortunate, especially since they may have had the same chances as people who chose differently. The writer Henry Thoreau said, "The mass of men will lead lives of quiet desperation. They will realize too late that they have not spent their time wisely."[3]

The satisfaction that comes with instant gratification is often fleeting. As with anything quickly acquired, it may quickly disappear. Satisfaction, gratification, happiness, joy and fulfillment are all things we commonly seek. Holding out for your prize could get you the greatest gift.

The Fruits of Delay

Satisfaction plotted over time takes on a very different trajectory when there is a planned delay in gratification. The graph has the same labels as the previous graph with Satisfaction and its various forms on the y-axis and Time on the x-axis. The person in this situation starts out at the same point as did the person in the instant gratification example. Their rise in satisfaction, however, is steady and predictable. They have a future focused state of mind. As they stay in school and study hard for their classes, they achieve satisfaction in the form of education, knowledge, confidence and skills that lead to competence in different areas. They grow in character and are successful in receiving excellent grades, academic rewards and recognition, part-time jobs, work-study programs and internships. They are on the road to reaching their dreams and getting the right job in the career they want.

(Satisfaction / Time)

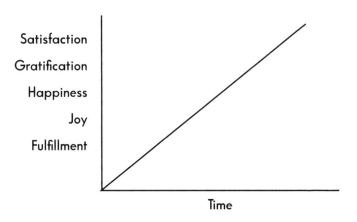

As they continue to grow in their jobs, they are developing their portfolio and a resume that will be desirable to many employers. Their strong job performance leads to raises in salary, bonuses and promotions. Their job becomes a career with promotions and salary increases. They are in a position with skills that will make them employable, even if the economy falls into bad times. They have a high level of satisfaction, gratification, happiness, joy and fulfillment over a longer period of time. This will place them in a better position than people in the first graph.

Ask yourself "Which graph do I want to represent my path to success? How badly do I want it?" Are you strong enough to wait and to do the work? Do you have the discipline and control? Would you rather have a short time of satisfaction or many years of greater control over your life and happiness? The choice is yours. You deserve the best, so work as if you believe this to be true. You can do it. As Henry Ford, the automobile company founder said, "If you think you can do a thing or if you think you can't do a thing, you're right."[4]

Four Directives to Influence Behavior

Since childhood, authority figures have delivered instructions designed to teach and guide you. Some of those lessons had the desired effect. In retrospect, however, you realize that the effectiveness of the messages varied based upon how they were delivered, your willingness to take instruction and a variety of other factors. Over the years, you have noticed remarkable similarities between the directives given in your youth and the requests made of you as an adult. Leaders and managers often give instructions coupled with some of the same memorable phrases that we first heard from our parents and teachers. The objective of these phrases is to elicit your compliance with their demands, commands or requests for action.

"Do as I say, because I said so"

People have used a variety of commands to get the kind of behavior they want. "Do as I say, because I said so," is the classic power phrase of authority. The person who utters this phrase usually has the power to administer rewards or punishment if someone fails to comply with their request. The sentence could just as easily end with, "or else." The boss, whether it is a supervisor, class instructor or a parent, expects that when they speak others will jump quickly into action. The person using this phrase does not wish to be questioned or challenged.

Frustrated parents and managers have used this phrase when they have run out of answers. When they are busy or in a hurry, they resort to this language to end conversations. They do not want to discuss the matter anymore. They want people to listen, obey and stay quiet. "Do as I say, because I said so," is a technique that can influence a number of people. When directed at the right individuals, it is a very effective means of getting a quick and desired response. It is useless, however, when delivered to the wrong person, for example, someone who has no fear of potential consequences for their failure to act.

"*Do as I say, not as I do*"

Some people adopt a hypocritical style to exert influence on others. They recognize that they do not have the discipline or integrity to practice what they preach. Yet, they insist that others listen to and obey their rules and commands. As in the case discussed above, this instruction is sometimes effective due to the power position of the speaker. However, the inconsistency and hypocrisy will render it ineffective in some cases. The resistant ones will not comply and they will use the leader's hypocrisy as justification for refusing to follow the commands. Or they will only follow the instructions when the leader is watching. They may even resent the perceived arrogance of one who expects others to do something that they are not committed to do. The advice may be solid, but the failure of the leader to lead by example may compromise the impact of the advice.

I recently read a powerful story about Mahatma Gandhi. The blog post, "Gandhi and the Boy Who Ate Too Much Sugar,"[5] tells of a mother's meeting with the influential leader.

A mother was desperate. Her son ate too much sugar — to the point that the mother was worried about his health. She had to do something. She tried everything. Nothing worked. She was out of ideas, save for one: maybe the boy's beloved idol could help.

One day the mother and the young boy set out on foot to go see the boy's idol. They walked for three hours, with a scorching hot sun bearing down upon them the entire way. Sweaty and exhausted, the mother and the boy finally reach their destination: the ashram of the boy's idol: Mahatma Gandhi.

"Bapu," the mother said, "Please help me convince my son to stop eating so much sugar. Please tell him how unhealthy it is for him." Gandhi looked at the mother, then at the boy. He took a moment to consider.

"Come back in three days," Gandhi said. "I will talk to your son then." As she wiped sweat from her brow, the mother nodded. She took the boy by the hand and they walked home.

Three days later, the mother and the boy made the same arduous trek back to see Gandhi. When they arrived, Gandhi was ready with his response. He looked at the boy. "Stop eating so much sugar," Gandhi said. "It is bad for your health."

The boy agreed. How could he not? One thousand requests from his mother could not equal this one from his idol. The mother was ecstatic. Her objective had been achieved. But she was perplexed nonetheless. "Bapu, thank you, but why could you not have said that three days ago?"

"I was not qualified to advise the boy. At that time, I too was eating lots of sugar."

Gandhi seemed to want a clear conscience and to only offer advice that he was willing to practice himself. In today's climate of transparency, it is difficult to present an image to the world while living a completely different life. Therefore, as leaders, we must be sure our actions match our words or run the risk of having only half-hearted followers who may not fully internalize the value of our advice.

"Don't do what I did — Learn from my mistakes"

We all know that experience is often the best teacher. Rebellion is a natural part of the human spirit. Rebellion also leads us to make mistakes from which we later learn valuable lessons. Many of us have received instruction, but elected to ignore it to listen to our own mind or the voices of others. Going down the wrong path has caused us discomfort and ultimately we realized we were wrong. Armed with the experience, we wish to let others know the value of staying on the right path. We do not want them to make the same errors in judgment that created avoidable hardships in our lives. We tell young people and others that we want to guide, "Do not do what I did. Learn from my mistakes."

This is sometimes seen as a tough love message or using scare tactics. Former prisoners have used a "scared straight" philosophy to convince young men and women to stay away from a life of crime. They feel that education on the negatives associated with criminal activity would discourage the youth from hanging with the wrong crowd and making questionable decisions. They take the glamour out of disobedience and use their lives as proof. Similarly, conversations within a corporation may involve older employees telling younger employees about the mistakes they themselves made early in their careers. These mentoring sessions or coaching moments are an effort to steer less tenured employees toward making better decisions on their career path. There is value in information sharing. That occurs when the different generations in the workplace tell their stories of arrival and survival within the context of the organization.

This approach also works on some people, but not on others. There will always be people who think they are too smart, clever, sophisticated, lucky, cool or too good-looking to suffer the consequences of their actions. They will view the sad story as something that only applies to others.

"*Do it like I did it – Follow my lead*"

This is normally a very potent approach. It is the "lead by positive example" model. People will look at you, your reputation and your execution and realize the value of your words and actions. Learning occurs through imitation or modeling behavior. "Let me show you how it's done" makes "Do it like I did it" an even more powerful instruction. Oftentimes, that phrase does not even need to be verbalized to have the desired effect. The power comes with seeing the leader act out the phrase. The practice that occurs, with or without the preaching, is what makes it work. It is the example exhibited on a day-to-day basis.

Leaders use phrases "Do it like I did it" and "Follow my example" to encourage positive behaviors that lead to desirable results. Keep in mind, however, that people also will imitate and follow negative leaders and negative examples. If the culture of an organization is rife with intimidation and a failure of leadership to show appreciation, individuals desiring to be leaders will notice the signals. They will emulate the same kind of insensitivity demonstrated by their leaders. As we discussed in Chapter 5, it is imperative to set high standards for yourself and to act with integrity and good character. Since your behavior as a leader will be imitated, you want that behavior to be positive and geared toward the growth of your peers and team members.

Leaders use each of these four directives to influence behavior to get individuals and groups to act and follow orders. They can each be effective in different circumstances. However, individually, we have found that they may not work on everyone all the time. Therefore, we must fully access the situation and the individuals involved to determine which directive to employ to get the best results.

Discussion Topics for Personal Reflection or Small Groups

1. Discuss a time when you a) delayed taking action until a more appropriate time and b) the result turned out better than if you had acted earlier.

2. Discuss the time someone told you that you would be a fine leader someday. What were the circumstances?

3. Has anyone ever told you that you could not do something or be somebody and you used that for motivation?

4. Have you ever given up because someone told you to quit? How did that make you feel and what have you done to prevent it from happening again?

5. For whom will you do your best work? Before you answer this question, consider the times in your life when you gave your best effort.

6. What leadership skills did you learn from your parents?

7. Which directives to influence behavior do you find yourself using most often?

CHAPTER 9

MAKE OTHERS BETTER

Elevate team performance by challenging and supporting the effort and results of peers

"I've learned that people will forget what you said, people will forget what you did, but people will never forget how you made them feel."

—Maya Angelou

"If your actions inspire others to dream more, learn more, do more and become more, you are a leader."

—John Quincy Adams

"If I can change your vocabulary and the content of your conversation; if I can infiltrate your language and cultivate your thoughts, I should be able to influence your behavior."

—Orlando Ceaser

People in Your Corner

The decision to make others better may be inspired by the people in your lives who unfailingly and unselfishly support your development. First, let us look at those individuals who want you to do better and to be better. These people are likely your relatives, friends or acquaintances. They may also include fellow students, co-workers, professors or supervisors. You may take their encouragement and support for granted, assuming that it is natural for those close to you to want the best for you.

Take a moment and list the people whom you feel are your genuine supporters. They are your allies, support network and cheerleaders. Write their names on a sheet of paper or log it into your computer. Take your time and think about all of the people in your life. Who are they? Go back to your childhood and review your current circumstances and associations. This list could grow in length very quickly. Review the list and your relationship to the person.

Now you have a list of people who want you to be successful. These are the people in your corner. You have a lot of people hoping that you will deliver your best and improve the situation in your family, community, country and planet. The actions you take to achieve your life's goals, the immediate and long-term ones, will have an impact on all of those who are in your corner. They will cheer you on and support you. They will also learn from observing your successes and missteps.

Newton's Cradle is a device used in science classes to demonstrate two of Sir Isaac Newton's laws of motion. The essence of Newton's first law is that an object at rest or in motion will remain at rest or in motion until acted upon by an outside force. Newton's third law teaches us that for every action there is an equal and opposite reaction.

The cradle consists of five metal balls, individually suspended from a rack and lined up. See Figure 1 below. When one of the end balls is pulled back and released, it strikes the next ball and sends energy through each ball in a chain reaction. The last ball picks up the energy and is pushed forward by the force of momentum. The last ball swings back as a pendulum and strikes the next ball. This sends the energy back across the other balls until it reaches the first ball and the cycle continues. If you release two balls, then two balls will be sent swinging at the other end. The more force used, the same force will move back and forth through the system.

Figure 1 Newton's Cradle

This model serves as an illustration for life and relationships. You affect other people by the way you live your life. At times, you will be a leader, a spark to begin an action. At other times, you will receive energy, messages and practices and you will have the responsibility to pass it along to the next person. This also relates to the Law of Reciprocity.

Another key to unlocking your leadership greatness is demonstrating your ability to elevate the performance of those around you. Superstars in sports have this ability. Michael Jordan is known for his skill in driving those around him to achieve their best results. He accomplished this through leading by example with his performance. He challenged, cajoled and pushed his teammates to be great as a team. The Chicago Bulls achieved six World Championships during Jordan's tenure in Chicago. He noticeably made the players around him a more cohesive unit. You have the same ability to enhance the performance of those around you by supporting, encouraging, challenging and holding each other accountable for results.

Managing Up

When you think of making others better, you think of your friends, coworkers, classmates or those who look up to you. You also have an opportunity to contribute to the performance of managers and professors. There is a concept called managing up, which means to manage the person or persons who are in positions above yours. Managing up is a relationship story. It is about establishing an effective working relationship with the manager, which allows you to meet your personal goals as well as the objectives of the manager and the organization. Ideally, you accomplish this dual goal by creating and energizing the climate for maximum productivity, proficiency and performance.

Managing up has several advantages. It allows you to have input into your career. Your managers and professors will have a significant impact on the direction of your career. They are in charge of grades, performance ratings, salary increases, promotions, mentoring, career guidance, personal growth, independent study projects, and other aspects of your academic and work life. The CARD approach (Compliance, Alliance, Reliance, and Defiance) is a useful tool for understanding how you can effectively use managing up strategies. Use of the term manager here is equally applicable to professors and anyone who is in a leadership role.

1. **Compliance** – The manager wants to ensure that you are doing your job well. You are conforming to the rules and regulations and exceeding personal and corporate objectives.

2. **Alliance** – You should form a partnership with your manager, one that focuses on team spirit, cooperation and a demonstrated desire to competently and proficiently complete the tasks at hand.

3. **Reliance** – They can count on you to do what you signed up to do. You are dependable and you look out for them. You present your manager with information that protects them. There are few surprises. You can be trusted and your loyalty is without question.

4. **Defiance** – You will not speak ill of the boss, sabotage their agenda or retaliate against them. You will not openly

challenge them in a meeting. If you have an issue, you will go to them in private. You are a cautious crusader for your own issues. You will pick your battles and challenge your manager when necessary. With any challenge, you will show your manager how any suggested changes will be to his or her advantage.

Organizations rely heavily on leaders at all levels and reward them for their commitment and contributions. When you use managing up techniques, your commitment to organizational goals will be visible and appreciated. Your leadership qualities will shine and will set you on track for greater opportunities within the organization. You will be called upon to instruct others and to demonstrate your secrets of excellence. By using the 10 Keys of leadership greatness discussed in this book, we push ourselves for the benefit of each member of the team, each manager we support, each student we influence, each customer we service and each stakeholder in the organization.

Teamwork and Leadership

A key to achieving your goals will be through working on a team. Organizations around the world recognize the value of teams in reaching goals. Some of the greatest accomplishments result from work performed in teams, from school projects to inter-departmental collaborations within businesses. You need to use teamwork techniques to help more people succeed. This involves learning more about individual members. They have different styles and ways of thinking and acting. Corralling the differences, while challenging at times, is well worth the effort. A diversity of ideas, arising from each member's unique perspective, contributes to a fresh approach to solving problems and a more comprehensive and creative solution.

Depending upon the size and composition of the team, you may need to act as the team leader. Your leadership greatness will be manifest by your ability to achieve lofty objectives by creating and leading highly productive teams. Whether in an academic setting or work environment, you will need a roadmap for managing the most effective teams. Consider the following five steps as a guide to framing your leadership objectives in a team setting.

Dreaming
- Involves the vision and seeing in your mind's eye the future reality
- Mission is the energy that powers your vision

Scheming
- The strategy and tactics used to achieve your objective
- The nuts and bolts, the road maps, plans and blueprint for success
- Rules, roles and regulations
- Standard operation procedures ("SOP's")

Screaming
- The tension and chaos you feel in the transformation
- The frustration and your reactions to the messiness
- Conflict as you confront the differences
- The pain of emptying yourself of the old ways

Teaming
- Trust is achieved
- The group functions as a unit
- Everyone is aware of their roles and goals
- Team members are individually committed to each other
- Individuals are aligned to a common purpose

Streaming
- Promoting — getting the word out
- Advertising your purpose and presence
- Networking to get better connected
- The Law of Reciprocity — you will receive what you transmit

When you work on a team, each member must help and challenge each other to improve. They must know the roles and goals of the unit and their responsibilities. As the team leader, you will be called upon to demonstrate your greatness, which will be defined by your results. By unlocking and unleashing the stored potential within you and your team, others will benefit from the wisdom of your words and the awesome acumen seen in your actions.

This chapter has focused on the ways making others better has far-reaching and lasting effects, even beyond your immediate success. You make others better in a myriad of ways, through team leadership, managerial support, encouragement, holding each other accountable, sharing ideas and standing as a symbol of excellence. As a result, you have cheerleaders, supporters, friends and team players who are on your side. This network or alliance will provide the necessary support and encouragement required today to be successful. As a result, together and individually, you will have clout and connections and can use your influence to make others better.

Discussion Topics for Personal Reflection or Small Groups

1. Who looks up to you? Who would be the president of your fan club?

2. What have you done to influence the performance of someone very close to you?

3. If you were putting together a team of your top five friends who would be on it?

4. Whom do you support with your time and resources?

5. Discuss your contributions to others. What have you done for others?

6. Describe a situation where you got on someone's good side for mutual benefit.

7. Describe the members of your inner circle. Describe how you help each other.

CHAPTER 10

SERVE OTHERS

*Willingness to volunteer and share
your talents and resources*

"I am of the opinion that my life belongs to the
community, and as long as I live, it is my privilege to
do for it whatever I can. I want to be thoroughly used
up when I die, for the harder I work, the more I live.
I rejoice in life for its own sake. Life is no brief candle
for me. It is a sort of splendid torch which I've got a
hold of for the moment, and I want to make it burn
as brightly as possible before handling it on to future
generations."

—George Bernard Shaw

"Being the richest man in the cemetery doesn't matter to
me...Going to bed at night saying we've done something
wonderful...That's what matters to me."

—Steve Jobs

"You give but little when you give of your possessions.
It is when you give of yourself that you truly give."

—Kahlil Gibran

Episodes of Serving

Dr. Martin Luther King Jr. said, "Everyone can be great because everyone can serve." You may have an image of a small child in a high chair wearing a bib. As an adult, you may have worn a bib yourself at a restaurant when eating particularly messy foods such as barbecue ribs and crab legs. In these situations, you were either being served or were serving yourself. I would like you to consider the image of removing the bib from around your neck and lowering it to your waist as an apron. This would signify that you are in a position to serve others.

After Hurricane Katrina struck New Orleans and the Gulf Coast, it took a while for the business community to get back on its feet. Astra Zeneca, the pharmaceutical company, chose to have its annual managers' meeting in New Orleans. It was the first large company to bring a meeting back to the area since the devastation. As a participant, I witnessed first hand the level of gratitude felt by the community. The people in New Orleans treated us like royalty. They were energized by our presence and commitment to the city. We hired local musicians to perform during our coffee breaks and at our evening functions. Many of them had not worked in months. We set aside one day to participate in community outreach activities such as painting various facilities and yard work. This was a great example of an organization reaching out to serve others.

Many corporations are proud of their social responsibility, as they give back to the community. They also support the volunteer efforts and projects of their employees. This is a powerful way of serving others and increases employee pride to be associated with such a caring organization. This also serves as a model to inspire employees to serve their fellow citizens in need.

A leadership principle that has been around for many years involves the classic pyramid. In the hierarchy of a company, the majority of the employees are at the base of the pyramid. As you move up the pyramid, the number of employees decreases. Finally, at the top of the pyramid sits the president or person in charge. Some organizations are implementing the concept of a reverse pyramid. Instead of all of the people at the base or lower levels working for the person at the top, you have the people at the top serving the employees at the lower level of the pyramid. When organizations implement this concept, there is a magical effect within the company. The front line employees do not feel as if they are working for upper management, but that upper management values their input as key contributors to the organization's success. An excellent example of this philosophy in action is the Nordstrom department store. In her article, "Your CEO is NOT the Top of the Pyramid," Michelle de Haaf discusses the great success Nordstrom has achieved by adopting the inverted pyramid philosophy, the centerpiece of their customer service and employee-centered ideology.[1]

Serving Others

Many people who volunteer their time and services to help others will tell of the positive feelings they personally experience. Some do it as an act of selflessness. They expect nothing in return, just the joy of helping their fellow citizen to get on their feet or to ease their suffering. Still others engage in acts of service with the desire to receive a reward or recognition for their gesture of kindness. The world needs both of these motives, for together they comfort those in need. The end justifies the means regardless of the motives in each situation.

Service activities may take you out of your comfort zone. There may be opportunities to serve in areas where may you feel unsafe. If you are prepared for that additional challenge, that is awesome. Acts of service do not have to be risky, however. There are plenty of service opportunities where safety is not an issue. You do not have to serve in a manner that makes you feel uncomfortable. Courage, therefore, should not be a condition of service. Whether you serve in a manner that makes you comfortable or uncomfortable, the world needs both types of service. There are people in need in most locations, under a variety of circumstances, who hunger for your assistance.

Opportunities may arise to provide service to others who have made bad decisions. There are also individuals whom life has dealt a series of complicated and unfortunate circumstances. You may be tempted to help one and not the other. In the back of your mind, you may want the first group to learn from their mistakes and make the right decisions to improve their circumstances. In an ideal world, you would not have to extend yourself. However, if they are currently in need you should address the need while applying the lesson.

Many fraternities, sororities, universities and communities have programs designed to serve those who are less fortunate than we are. Participation in the serving opportunities is an excellent way to demonstrate leadership and model expectations. Paying back or paying forward has a healing effect on those individuals who benefit from your acts of generosity.

Serving others should also be the mindset you have when approaching people at networking events. Rather than dominating the conversation with all of your achievements and background, open with something focused on the other person. Ask the question, "What can I do for you?" Alternatively, lead with elements from your background that could help them:

- Meet a key person who could help them

- Find key information on jobs or internships

- Provide the names of services that could benefit their job search

You may achieve these objectives by listening to them tell you their story and acting accordingly to provide service.

Your objective is to unlock your leadership greatness. When you are on life's leadership journey and when you achieve leadership milestones, serving others will be an integral part of your storyline. You will regularly enhance and enrich the lives of citizens of our world. You will give them confidence in humankind, as you strive to improve the human condition through service and compassion.

Additionally, as a leader, it is important to show your willingness to serve others. In your leadership capacity, you will always be an example for those who look up to you to and have high expectations and belief in your abilities. Let them see your kindness. Let them share in your generosity and benefit from your concern.

How do you plan your serving opportunities? How do you make it a regular part of your weekly routine? The following are some ways that you can make service to others an integral part of your life:

- Carry extra money (loose change) with you for situations when you encounter people who are down and out

- Pick a certain day of the week to volunteer at a food pantry, soup kitchen or other establishment that helps the poor

- Participate in fraternity, sorority or your university's civic projects

- Contact service organizations such as the YMCA, YWCA, Salvation Army and local churches, synagogues, temples, mosques and nonprofit organizations for opportunities to serve

- Develop a program around your passion for helping those in need. This could involve collecting clothing, shoes and canned goods to deliver to worthy charities

"To whom much is given much is expected." By exercising your leadership gifts, you will unlock your leadership greatness. You will ease the discomfort and hard times experienced by many. The level of poverty and injustice among the people, who are less fortunate, will be diminished by your positive acts of grace.

Discussion Topics for Personal Reflection or Small Groups

1. Describe a time when you did something for someone else without the expectation of personal benefit.

2. Discuss your volunteer activities.

3. Make a list of the organizations with which you would like to serve.

4. Who are the people you admire and how do they help others?

5. What are your thoughts about those who are less fortunate than you are?

NOTES

Chapter 1 — Be Fit for the Role

1. Giuseppe Novelli, "Personalized Genomic Medicine," *Internal and Emergency Medicine* 5 (Issue 1 Supplement) (2010): pp. 81-90, doi: 10.1007/s11739-010-0455-9.

2. Martin Meredith, *Born in Africa: The Quest for the Origins of Human Life.* (New York: PublicAffairs, 2011).

3. "What's the body worth," *Liblog: Newsletter of the Mayo Clinic Libraries*, Jan 14, 2010, http://liblog.mayo.edu/2010/01/14/whats-the-body-worth/.

4. Dr. Wayne W. Dyer, *The Shift* (Carlsbad, California: Hay House, Inc., 2010).

5. Dr. Wayne W. Dyer, *The Shift* (Carlsbad, California: Hay House, Inc., 2010).

6. You can take The Meyers-Briggs assessment online at **www.capt.org/take-mbti-assessment/mbti.htm.** The DISC profile is also available online at **www.onlinediscprofile.com.**

7. Sheldon Ceaser, M.D., *The Most Powerful Book of Affirmations Ever Written* (Chicago: Sheldon T. Ceaser, M.D., INC., 2013).

Chapter 2 — Be Powered By A Dream

1. Napoleon Hill, *Think and Grow Rich* (Greenwich, Conn.: Fawcett Crest, 1960).

2. Dr. Wayne W. Dyer, *The Shift* (Carlsbad, California: Hay

House, Inc., 2010).

Chapter 3 – Be A Student Of The Game

1. Jon Gordon, *The No Complaining Rule: Positive Ways to Deal with Negativity at Work* (Hoboken, New Jersey: John Wiley & Sons, 2008).

2. Merriam-Webster Dictionary, www.merriam-webster.com/dictionary/conform.

3. "Larry Bird Quotes," *Brainy Quote*, p.1, http//www.brainyquote.com/quote/authors/l/larry_bird.html.

4. James Malinchak, *Big Money Speaker Bootcamp*, www.bigmoneyspeaker.com.

Chapter 4 – Master The Fundamentals

1. Dr. Martin E.P. Seligman, Learned Optimism (New York: Knopf, 1991).

2. Earl Nightingale in his recording The Strangest Secret. (www.learnoutloud.com/Catalog/Wealth/The-Strangest-Secret/47127).

3. "William James Quote," Great-Quotes, http://www.great-quotes.com/quote/74039.

4. Quote from George Bernard Shaw's 1902 play, "Mrs. Warren's Profession" (Toronto: University of Toronto Libraries, 2011).

5. Orlando Ceaser quote from speeches on "How to be an Impact Player."

6. Dr. Philip Zimbardo, and Nikita Duncan Coulombe, The Demise of Guys: Why Boys are Struggling and What We

Can Do About It (Amazon Digital Services, Inc, 2012).

7. Malcolm Gladwell, Outliers: The Story of Success (New York: Little, Brown and Company, 2008).

8. Alan Lakein, How to get Control of Your Time and Your Life (New York: Signet, 1989).

9. Robert J. Kriegel and Louis Palter, If It Ain't Broke...Break It (New York: Warner Books, Inc., 1992).

10. David Lambert, Body Language 101 (Canada: Skyhorse Publishing, 2008).

11. DDI (Development Dimensions International), www.ddiworld.com.

12. Linda Cattelan, "The S.O.A.R. Answer Model," Human Resources, 2012, http://www.humanresources.com/491/the-soar-answer-model/.

Chapter 5 – Set High Standards

1. Colin Powell, My American Journey (New York: Random House, 1995).

2. This quote has been widely attributed to Mark Twain. See, "Father," twainquoutes, http://www.twainquotes.com/Father.html.

3. Jim Rohn, The Art of Exceptional Living (Audio CD – Abridged) (New York: Simon & Schuster Audio, 2003).

4. Abraham Maslow, "Hierarchy of Needs," NetMba Business Knowledge Center, http://www.netmba.com/mgmt/ob/motivation/maslow/.

5. William Ernest Henley, "Invictus," The Poetry Foundation,

http://www.poetryfoundation.org/poem/182194.

6. Dr. Wayne W. Dyer, The Shift (Carlsbad, California: Hay House, Inc., 2010).

7. Atul Gawande, The Checklist Manifesto (New York: Metropolitan Books, 2009),

8. Tony Alessandra delivered the referenced speech at the annual meeting for the Society for Pharmaceuticals and Biotech Trainers at the Intercontinental Hotel, San Diego, CA, 1987.

Chapter 6 – Always Be Creative (ABC)

1. Dewitt Jones, Everyday Creativity. Videotape series distributed by Star Thrower Distribution of St. Paul, MN.

2. "Linus Pauling Quotes," IZ Quotes, accessed May 12, 2015, http://izquotes.com/quote/296491.

3. Roger Von Oech, Whack on the Side of the Head (25th Anniversary edition) (New York: Warner Books, 2008).

4. "Fosbury Flops to an Olympic Record," http://www.history.com/this-day-in-history/fosbury-flops-to-an-olympic-record.

Chapter 7 – Execute With Passion

1. Larry Bossidy and Ram Charan, *Execution* (New York: Crown Business, 2002).

2. Jack Welch and Suzy Welch, *Winning* (New York: Harper Business, 2005).

3. Jim Collins, *Good to Great* (New York: Harper Business, 2001).

Chapter 8 — Lead By Example

1. Richard Arum and Josipa Roksa, Academically Adrift: Limited Learning on College Campuses (Chicago: University of Chicago Press, 2010).

2. Andrew McAfee, "Alarming Research Shows the Sorry State of US Higher Ed," Harvard Business Review, July 13, 2013, https://hbr.org/2013/07/alarming-research-shows-sorry.

3. Henry Thoreau, Walden, or Life in the Woods (Virginia: Wilder Publications, 2008).

4. Henry Ford Quotes," Brainy Quotes, http://www. brainyquote.com/quotes/quotes/h/henryford122817.htm,

5. "Gandhi and the Boy Who Ate Too Much Sugar," Primility, June 3, 2014, http://primility.com/gandhi-and-the-boy-who-ate-too-much-sugar/.

Chapter 10 — Serve Others

1. Michelle de Haaf, "Your CEO is NOT the Top of the Pyramid," Medallia, June 17, 2014, blog.medallia.com/customer-experience/ceo-top-pyramid/.

ABOUT ORLANDO CEASER

Orlando Ceaser is a prolific writer and professional speaker for Watchwell Communications, Inc., www.watchwellinc.com. He spent his first career as a business executive in the pharmaceutical industry. He has extensive experience in sales, management, training, diversity, marketing, leadership and personal development. As a Sales Leader, he led an organization of 700 people.

Mr. Ceaser advises students and employees to become Impact Players in school, work and in their communities to achieve better results. His audiences are comprised of business leaders, corporate executives, entrepreneurs, employees and students. He is the author of Unlock your Leadership Greatness – For Students, Unlock your Diversity Greatness and The Isle of Knowledge and a book of poetry entitled Leadership Above the Rim – The Poetry of Possibility. His blog, The "O" Zone, www.myozonelayer.com, focuses on management and leadership.

Mr. Ceaser has published articles on career development, interviewing, management, leadership and selling. His words have appeared in articles in Financial Times, Human Resource Executive, The Scientist, The Boston Globe, The Chicago Defender, and Pharmaceutical Representative Magazine. His comic strips, Cocky and Rhodette and Cocky, Jr., focus on life in the corporate world and through the eyes of a student.

Mr. Ceaser and his wife reside in South Barrington, Illinois.

Notes:

Notes:

Notes: